L I V I N G
True

May the God of hope fill you with all joy and peace
as you trust in him, so that you may overflow
with hope by the power of the Holy Spirit.

ROMANS 15:13

LIVING

40 DAYS TO GET
BACK TO YOU

CHRISTY WRIGHT

RAMSEY
PRESS

Published by Ramsey Press, The Lampo Group, LLC
Franklin, Tennessee 37064

This publication is designed to provide accurate and authoritative information with regard to the subject matter covered. It is sold with the understanding that the publisher is not engaged in rendering financial, accounting, or other professional advice. If financial advice or other expert assistance is required, the services of a competent professional should be sought.

Unless otherwise noted, Scripture quotations are from the Holy Bible, New International Version®, NIV®, Copyright © 1973, 1978, 1984, 2011 by Biblica, Inc.® Used by permission of Zondervan. All rights reserved worldwide.

All Scripture marked NRSV is from the New Revised Standard Version Bible, copyright © 1989 the Division of Christian Education of the National Council of the Churches of Christ in the United States of America. Used by permission. All rights reserved.

All Scripture marked ESV is from The ESV® Bible (The Holy Bible, English Standard Version®). ESV® Text Edition: 2016. Copyright © 2001 by Crossway, a publishing ministry of Good News Publishers. The ESV® text has been reproduced in cooperation with and by permission of Good News Publishers. Unauthorized reproduction of this publication is prohibited. All rights reserved.

The Holy Bible, English Standard Version (ESV) is adapted from the Revised Standard Version of the Bible, copyright Division of Christian Education of the National Council of the Churches of Christ in the U.S.A. All rights reserved.

All Scripture marked NASB is from the NEW AMERICAN STANDARD BIBLE®, Copyright © 1960, 1962, 1963, 1968, 1971, 1972, 1973, 1975, 1977, 1995 by The Lockman Foundation. Used by permission.

All Scripture marked NCV is from the New Century Version®. Copyright © 2005 by Thomas Nelson. Used by permission. All rights reserved.

All Scripture marked NLT is taken from the Holy Bible, New Living Translation, copyright © 1996, 2004, 2015 by Tyndale House Foundation. Used by permission of Tyndale House Publishers, Inc., Carol Stream, Illinois 60188. All rights reserved.

All Scripture marked NKJV is taken from the New King James Version®. Copyright © 1982 by Thomas Nelson. Used by permission. All rights reserved.

All Scripture marked NLV is from Scripture quotations marked NLV are taken from the New Life Version, copyright © 1969 and 2003. Used by permission of Barbour Publishing, Inc., Uhrichsville, Ohio 44683. All rights reserved.

All Scripture marked CSB is from The Christian Standard Bible. Copyright © 2017 by Holman Bible Publishers. Used by permission. Christian Standard Bible®, and CSB® are federally registered trademarks of Holman Bible Publishers, all rights reserved.

ISBN: 978-1-9421-2116-9

Editors: Jennifer Day and Rachel Knapp
Cover Design: Chris Carrico and Gretchen Hyer
Interior Design: Gretchen Hyer and Kristin Goble

Printed in the United States of America
20 21 22 23 24 WLS 5 4 3 2 1

MY PRAYER FOR YOU

Father God, this devotional is dedicated to my friend holding this book right now. Meet her exactly where she is and speak to her in a way that only you can. In the forty days ahead, give her a peace that surpasses all understanding and a confidence that can only come from you. As she goes on this journey back to herself, may she not only have a deeper insight of who she was created to be, but also a deeper connection with you as her creator. Thank you for her and for all you're going to do in her and through her. Amen.

CONTENTS

CONTENTS

Section 2: Who You Are

Section 3: Where You Are

CONTENTS

Section 4: Where You're Going

INTRODUCTION

I'm really uncomfortable right now, but let's face it, I'm really uncomfortable a lot these days. It's not a cause for concern and, actually, it's completely normal. As I write this, I have a baby girl being formed in my ever-growing belly. She's relocating my organs, squishing my lungs, and compressing my blood vessels. It sounds crazy, of course, but it's all completely normal.

Here's the thing, though: I don't *feel* normal. I am so unbelievably grateful to be pregnant. It's not lost on me what an amazing gift that is. And at the same time, I don't feel like myself.

This is my third baby, and you'd think I'd be able to roll with it by now. But when your body is doing new, weird (and often unattractive) things every single day, and you feel like you have no control over what you can and can't do, it's hard to get used to—regardless of how many times you've been through it.

And don't get me started on the feelings. I'm feeling overwhelmed and excited and nervous and, let's be honest, a little crazy. I'm feeling so grateful and uncomfortable and frustrated—and then I feel guilty for feeling uncomfortable and frustrated. I have so many feelings that even my feelings have feelings!

The bottom line is this: *I don't feel like myself.*

This is one of the many times in my life that I've not felt like myself.

I also didn't feel like myself when I was working eighty hours a week at a nonprofit—pouring myself into my career right after graduating college.

I didn't feel like myself when I was single in my twenties—trying to figure out who I was when everyone around me seemed to be the exact thing that I *wasn't*: married.

I didn't feel like myself when I volunteered to speak to college students all over the country when I'd never spoken publicly in my life—trying something new and terrifying and feeling like a complete fraud.

I haven't felt like myself countless times since my first son, Carter, and then my second son, Conley, were born—losing myself in my role as their mom like so many of us do.

I've lost myself in my work, my relationships, my goals, and in different seasons of life.

And all I wanted anytime that happened was one thing: *to simply get back to me.*

The Questions Our Hearts Are Asking

Get back to me. Those words were always the words I felt. I don't even know if I knew what that meant, but in different moments of desperation, I knew I wanted it. I knew I needed it. There was something I was missing and thirsting for.

Those are also the words I've heard from thousands of women across this country as I've spent time speaking, coaching, and visiting with them over the last ten years. "I just want to get back to me." "I feel like I've lost myself." "I don't know who I am anymore." "I feel stuck." They say it in different ways again and again.

Maybe you've been there before and maybe you're there now. Maybe there's a part of you that feels lost—or at least pushed to the back corner of your life collecting dust. Maybe you're overwhelmed or unfulfilled or both. Maybe you're so busy you don't even know who you are or how you feel because you're just trying to keep your head above water. Maybe you've felt limited by labels others have given you, or more commonly, labels you've unconsciously given yourself. Maybe you're feeling lost in life or maybe you're just plain tired. I've been in all of those places. I still find myself there at times.

That yearning and longing to get back to ourselves draws out some intimidating but really important questions. We start to wonder . . .

Who am I outside of my work or caring for my children?
Where do I find my identity if it's not as my husband's wife and children's mom?

3

Who was I before life got so ... busy?
Am I doing the right things?
What is my purpose in this world?

And the question that can be one of the scariest of all: *What do I want for my life?*

Believe it or not, friend, God has a lot to say about all of those things. That's why I'm so excited to begin this journey with you—spending forty days getting back to you so that you can live true to who you are.

This Is for You

This devotional is just for you. It's not a random book for an obligatory quiet time. I don't want it to be something you dread doing or feel guilty about when you miss a day. It's not meant to be a burden or become just another thing on your endless to-do list. It's *for you*.

Here's what that means: Reading this devotional is not something you're doing *for God*, to please him or earn brownie points. It's not something you're doing to impress others. It's not something you're doing because anyone is making you. This is one thing in your life that is 100 percent for you. Just you. That might feel weird and selfish to say (and we'll talk more about all of those feelings and more in the pages ahead) but it's true. It's for you.

We're going to spend forty days together going on a journey to get back to you.

I believe that before your husband or your kids or your job or your many roles and responsibilities, you had a set of gifts, dreams, and desires that you offered the world. If we aren't careful, we stop offering who we are and instead just become what the world needs us to be: a warm meal on the table, a ride to soccer, a task completed.

But friend, you are so much more than that. You are more than your roles and responsibilities. You are more than completed tasks. *You are more.* And I believe God is inviting you to discover what that "more" really is.

The Journey Ahead

What would it look like to stop feeling paralyzed by insecurity and doubt and instead find confidence in who you are and who God created you to be? Imagine living your day with a heart and mind full of faith, not fear. What if you stopped feeling overwhelmed and started actually having fun? How amazing would it be if you reconnected to who you were before life got busy and you got lost in the mix? I think those are just a few of the possibilities that lie ahead for you on this journey.

There are four things we need to understand if we're going to get back to who God created us to be and—even more—to become the best and truest version of that. Let's talk about each of them.

Who God Is

Before we can explore who you are, we need to reset on who God is. It's easy to let outside influences like the media, life experiences, past hurts, or even well-meaning family and friends shape who we believe God to be. Sometimes those influences are unbelievably helpful, and other times, they create a false image in our mind about God—an image that affects our relationship with him and our life. But thankfully, the Bible, God's Word to us, has a lot to say about who God is. We're going to spend the first ten days of our journey studying and understanding what the Bible says about who God is and what that means for our lives.

Who You Are

After we reset on who God is, we're going to spend the next ten days exploring who we are in him. If our identity is not found in our roles, responsibilities, and relationships, then where is it found? What makes up who we are? What are the sources of our identity? Which ones are healthy and which ones are harmful? We're going to dive into all of the (amazing!) things that make you *you*, and you'll remember—or maybe learn for the first time—what God says about you.

Where You Are

Life is made up of seasons. It's so easy to let the season you're in define not only how you feel, but also who you are. We're going to spend ten days exploring the season you're in and how this can affect each of the different areas of your life, like your family, your home, and your money. You might have a giant belly and not be able to put on your own shoes like me right now, or your house might be a disaster because you have three young kids at home, or you might be scraping pennies together to get by—but these are examples of *where* you are, not *who* you are. You are not the season you're in. When you know who God is and who you are in him, you can find strength and grace for your current season, regardless of how it looks at the time.

You are not the season you're in.

Where You're Going

In the last stage of our journey, we'll spend ten days looking ahead to where you're going. I know that past wounds and difficult present circumstances can make us want to give up hope. We might not say that outright, but the sentiment is the same:

"I don't want to get my hopes up."
"I'll believe it when I see it."
"I'm just being realistic."

We might put all of those statements under the banner of being a practical grown-up, but the reality is, we're playing it safe and protecting ourselves from pain. Our God *is* the God of hope. He doesn't ask us to know the details of how things are going to work out, but he does ask us to trust him that they will.

So this last stage of our journey is all about building a bold faith that believes God is who he says he is and that he can do what he says he'll do. By this point, we'll have spent time remembering who God is, recovering who you are, and understanding the season you're in. And now it's time to cultivate confidence in the God who created you and the future he has for you.

He's leading you somewhere, friend, and he wants your unconditional, surrendered faith in him—regardless of how impractical, illogical, or irrational it may seem. That's what faith is, after all, isn't it? *"Now faith is confidence in what we hope for and assurance about what we do not see"* (Hebrews 11:1). You can't see where God is leading you, and I can't either. But because we know who God is and who we are in him, we can have confidence—certainty—in our future.

I'm excited and honored to take this journey with you. I pray it's one where God shows up in ways you don't expect, busts out of boxes you didn't even know you'd put him in, and transforms your life in a way that is truly more than you could ever ask or imagine.

This is just a little book in your hands. I know that. But when God gets involved, seas are parted, walls fall, chains are broken, and lives are forever changed. That's my prayer for you in the pages and days ahead. That's my prayer for all of us as we continue on this faith walk together.

Are you ready to get back to you?

Let's do this!

Who God Is

It seems like I'm always on the go. Are you like that? I'm always carrying fifteen different bags and trying to do at least three things at one time, all the time. One of the things I'm notorious for multitasking is makeup. I can put on lipstick while scrambling eggs or rub in my foundation furiously with my fingertips while tossing dirty laundry into the hamper. I often end up throwing a few of my last makeup items into my purse as I rush out the door to be finished somewhere between my house and my destination.

But the same thing always happens when I do this. When I go to finish up the final steps of my makeup routine, I open up the small compact of powder and try to look into the tiny mirror to see what I'm doing. But because the compact has been tossed and turned, it has powder all over the mirror and it's a huge mess. I can't see myself, and I definitely can't see what I'm doing. I try to wipe it off with my finger—in a rush, of course—but I never feel like I can really see myself.

That's what it's like when we try to figure out who we are or what we're doing without fully understanding who God is. It's like trying to look in a clouded, blurry mess of a reflection. Maybe your image of God got messy when you experienced a tragedy in your life. You can't imagine how God could be good when he let you go through *that.* Maybe your view of God has been distorted by the competing theologies and opinions thrown at you over the years. Maybe you've never had any ideas about God at all, so you don't even know what to look for.

Regardless of how you might have gotten off track over the years, if you're going to get back to yourself, you have to first have a clear mirror to look into. You need to be able to see who you are as a reflection of God. Genesis 1:27 says, *"So God created human-kind in his image, in the image of God he created them; male and female he created them"* (NRSV). Since you are made in the image of God, and this is a journey to get back to you, you first need to have an accurate image of God—one that can only come from God directly through his Word.

In this first part of our journey, we're going to look at ten different attributes of God. These are ten things God says about himself—so we know they're true. These first ten days are going to help us wipe the blurry mess off our image of him so we can see him—and later, ourselves—more clearly.

God Is Good

"You are good, and what you do is good."
—Psalm 119:68

I remember when I applied for that camp director job—the job I knew I was going to get. I had been recruited for it, and I was more than qualified. I was so burnt out on my current position and could not wait for a new challenge. I interviewed in the winter in heels and a real suit, and I just knew I nailed it. Everything was lining up perfectly. I was positive God was orchestrating this.

That's why I was that much more devastated when I got the call informing me I didn't get it. I was stunned. I tried to stop my voice from shaking on the phone as I mustered something about how I understood and was grateful for the opportunity. And the moment I hung up, I lost it. I couldn't believe it. I was more than qualified for this job. It was exactly what I wanted, and it was the pay raise I desperately needed.

I lay on my couch and cried angry tears. I thought, *How could God do this? I thought he was good? I thought he wanted good things for me?* Then I tried to comfort myself in the only way I knew how: I took matters into my own hands. I picked up my computer and started frantically searching job openings. This was one of the *many* times in my life I've doubted God's goodness and taken matters into my own hands. And that, friend, is actually how sin first entered the world.

In Genesis, when Adam and Eve are in the Garden of Eden minding their own business, it's the serpent who first suggested that God might not be good.

Now the serpent was more crafty than any of the wild animals the LORD God had made. He said to the woman, "Did God really say, 'You must not eat from any tree in the garden'?" The woman said to the serpent, "We may eat fruit from the trees in the garden, but God did say, 'You must not eat fruit from the tree that is in the middle of the garden, and you must not touch it, or you will die.'"

"You will not certainly die," the serpent said to the woman. "For God knows that when you eat from it your eyes will be opened, and you will be like God, knowing

*good and evil." When the woman saw that the fruit
of the tree was good for food and pleasing to the eye,
and also desirable for gaining wisdom, she took some
and ate it. She also gave some to her husband, who
was with her, and he ate it."* (Genesis 3:1–6)

This entire passage can be summarized with: They took matters into their own hands. It's what I do all the time. I doubt God's goodness and take matters into my own hands. But we know how this plays out:

*Then the eyes of both of them were opened, and
they realized they were naked; so they sewed fig
leaves together and made coverings for themselves.*
(Genesis 3:7)

For the first time ever, shame entered the picture.

Oh, Eve must have thought. *I thought I had this. I thought I knew better. I thought my way was best.* But instead, she was exposed and ashamed. I don't know about you, but I've been there plenty of times when my "best" plans blow up in my face.

God will guide us in ways we don't understand. But that's why we have to remember that God is good all the time. Even when it seems like he's holding out on you, he's not. Even when it seems like you definitely know better, you don't. The Bible reminds us again and again that God is good:

Give thanks to the LORD, for he is good; his love endures forever. (Psalm 107:1)

The Lord is good to all; he has compassion on all he has made. (Psalm 145:9)

No good thing does [God] withhold from those whose walk is blameless. (Psalm 84:11)

When God tells us something in the Bible repeatedly, it means it's *really* important for us to get. This battle isn't new. It's the same high-stakes lie the enemy has told us since the beginning. And when we believe that lie, it doesn't turn out well—it never has. As we begin this journey, we need to begin with the most basic truth about God: *He is good.*

REFLECTION AND PRAYER

Do you believe God is good? How do you remember he's good when it doesn't feel like it? How can you resist the temptation to take matters into your own hands and let him lead instead?

Spend some time in prayer today asking God to give you a peace that surpasses all understanding as you trust that he is good.

GOD IS
Good

God Is with Us

"Be strong and courageous. Do not be frightened,
and do not be dismayed,
for the LORD your God is with you wherever you go."
—JOSHUA 1:9 (ESV)

*I*t was chaotic and terrifying and surreal.

I remember the moment my doctor pushed the red button on my hospital bed that signaled fifteen other medical professionals to come running into the delivery room. I remember when the doctors stopped talking to me and started speaking only to each other, as if I wasn't there. I remember when someone yelled, "Get the husband out of here!" I remember the fluorescent hospital lights zooming over my head like dashed white interstate lines as they ran, pushing my bed to the operating room. I remember trying to help the doctors get my body onto the operating table using only my arms because I couldn't feel anything from the torso down. I wanted to do anything I could to speed up whatever was going on. And I had no idea what was going on.

What transpired next was an emergency C-section. Carter had an umbilical cord prolapse cutting off his blood supply, which led to his heart rate plummeting instantly. Thankfully, the surgeons and nurses got him out and he was fine. But I didn't know that. Carter wasn't crying and, still, no one was talking to me—no matter how many questions I asked.

I was lying on the table terrified when another doctor in head-to-toe scrubs rushed through the double swinging doors straight over to me yelling, "I'm here, I'm here, I'm *heeere!*" I was already scared out of my mind, and now some psychotic doctor was coming at me—and I was helpless on the table to do anything about it. He got about an inch from my face repeating those same words, "I'm HERE!"

With wide, wild eyes and in complete confusion and terror, I yelled back at him, "WHO ARE YOU?"

"It's me! Matt!"

It was my husband.

Because he was wearing surgical scrubs with a mask and cap, I had no idea who he was. Once Carter was delivered safely, the doctors had let Matt come into the operating room to be with me. So who I thought was a terrifying stranger was actually someone who loved me more than anyone in the world. My person was right there with me—literally one inch from my face!—and I couldn't see it.

Fear does that to us sometimes, doesn't it? We can't see clearly because we're afraid and confused.

One of my favorite stories in the Bible is when Jesus walks out to his disciples on the water. Keep in mind that these are men who knew Jesus well. They had spent a lot of time together and loved each other. Yet, when Jesus came walking on the water in the middle of the night, they felt like I did: helpless, confused, and terrified.

> *Shortly before dawn Jesus went out to them, walking on the lake. When the disciples saw him walking on the lake, they were terrified. "It's a ghost," they said, and cried out in fear.* (Matthew 14:25-26)

This story is a good reminder that when we're in a terrifying situation, or when life is just hard and exhausting, God is with us—even when it doesn't seem like it. In fact, when he sent his son to earth for us, he named him *Immanuel* which means *"God with us"* (Matthew 1:23). We are never alone.

And unlike Matt, God isn't held up behind operating room doors waiting to enter. God isn't far away in the clouds peering down when he's not busy doing something more important. He's with us every minute of every day of our lives. Psalm 139:7–10 says, *"Where can I go from your Spirit? Where can I flee from your presence? . . . If I rise on the wings of the dawn, if I settle on the far side of the sea, even there your hand will guide me, your right hand will hold me fast."* I love this reminder. So, when we're scared and confused—like I was during my C-section or like the disciples were in the boat—we can take comfort in the fact that God is always, *always* with us.

REFLECTION AND PRAYER

Where in your life do you feel confused, scared, or helpless? What does it mean to you that you're not alone—that God is with you in every situation?

Spend some time in prayer today asking God to help you recognize his presence in the midst of what you're going through.

God Is Faithful

"The one who calls you is faithful and he will do it."
—1 Thessalonians 5:24

I remember when Jenny called me crying, heartbroken that her relationship with Hunter was over. They had dated for two and a half years, and we all thought he was *the one*. They lived in separate cities, and just when Jenny was willing to move and leave her amazing job, house, church, and friends in Nashville to be with him in Pittsburg, it ended. Jenny was crushed. And the idea of starting over in her thirties only made it hurt more. "What is God *doing*?" she cried.

What Jenny and I didn't know when we talked that day was that just two months later, God would bring someone from her past back into her life who would become her husband. She would be engaged four months later and married three months after that.

And if that isn't crazy enough, Jenny would have to move because her husband's job was taking him across the country—to Hawaii. That's right. Six days after marrying her amazing husband, she was living in paradise with him.

When Jenny tells this story, all she can talk about is how faithful God is—from preparing her to leave her life in Nashville way ahead of time (for Hawaii, not Pittsburg!) to every other detail in her story.

When you read the Bible, you also see example after example of God's faithfulness. We doubt, and God is still faithful. We waver, and God stays steady. We stray, and God stays close. We give up, and God keeps going. Romans 3:3–4 says, *"What if some were unfaithful? Will their unfaithfulness nullify God's faithfulness? Not at all!"* Again and again, God shows us that regardless of what we do or don't do, he is faithful.

For example, in Genesis, God told Abraham that Sarah would become pregnant with a son, even though she was way past childbearing age.

I will bless her and will surely give you a son by her. . . . she will be the mother of nations; kings of peoples will come from her. (Genesis 17:16)

Do you know what Abraham did at this point? He did what I would probably do. He laughed!

Abraham fell facedown; he laughed and said to himself, "Will a son be born to a man a hundred years

old? Will Sarah bear a child at the age of ninety?"
(Genesis 17:17)

And it wasn't just Abraham laughing. Later, when Sarah overheard what God said to Abraham, she laughed too. God's response to Abraham and Sarah is a good reminder for us today.

*The Lord said to Abraham, "Why did Sarah laugh
and say, 'Will I really have a child, now that I am old?'
Is anything too hard for the LORD? I will return to you
at the appointed time next year and Sarah will have a
son." (Genesis 18:13–14)*

And I'm sure you know what happened: God was faithful and came through in spite of their unbelief.

He was faithful then, and he is still faithful today. Our God is a God who comes through for you. Not every now and then: Every. Single. Time. God doesn't come through for you because *you* deserve it. God comes through for you because that's who *he* is.

God comes through for you because that's who *he* is.

I don't know what dreams you're dreaming or prayers you're praying, but I want you to know that our God is faithful. He's not a mean, vindictive God who builds you up only to pull the rug out from under you. He's a God who comes through for you. It may not be in the way you expect. It may not be in the way you prefer. But he will not abandon you. If he said it, he will do it!

REFLECTION AND PRAYER

Where might you be holding back or playing it safe because you're not sure God will come through? What has God invited you to do that sounds so impossible it made you laugh in disbelief? Think back over the past twelve months. How have you seen God's faithfulness in your life? You can even journal your answer to capture how he's been faithful.

Spend some time in prayer today asking God to help you believe that just as he was faithful before, he will be faithful again.

DAY 4

God Is All-Knowing

---

*"Your eyes saw my unformed body; all the days
ordained for me were written in your book before one
of them came to be."*

—Psalm 139:16

My boys do the most amazing thing. They've both done it since they were babies, before they could even walk or talk. Granted, all children do this, so that may make it seem a little less amazing to some people. But not to me because, of course, they are mine.

When something new, loud, or frightening happens near them, their first reaction is to look at me. When the mailman bangs on the door, Carter gets scared and looks at me. When a storm is rolling through and the lightning cracks and the thunder shakes all around us, Conley gets scared and looks at me. Anytime something scares either one of them, my sons look at me.

When they look at me, their eyes are searching my face for the answer to their question: *Is everything okay? Is everything okay, Mom? Are we safe, Mom? Am I going to be alright, Mom? Do you know what's going on, Mom? Have you got this under control, Mom?*

And the moment we lock eyes and I smile and assure them in an upbeat, confident tone that everything is okay, all of their fears are swept away. I've got this and, most of all, I've got them.

One day a while back, a garbage truck made a loud, banging noise outside and Conley looked at me for reassurance. As I picked him up and comforted him in my arms, I felt God say to me, *That's how you know things are okay, Christy. You don't look at the scary things around you; you look at me.*

As adults, we often don't know what's going on in our lives. Instead, we walk around like little children who have just been frightened by something out of our control. We don't understand what's going on and that scares us.

We might not know what's going on, and we certainly don't know what's going to happen tomorrow, but here's the thing: We do know the one who knows. We can rest in the truth that God is all-knowing. This is all over the Bible:

You have searched me, LORD, and you know me. You know when I sit and when I rise; you perceive my thoughts from afar. You discern my going out and my lying down; you are familiar with all my ways. Before a word is on my tongue you, LORD, know it completely. (Psalm 139:1–4)

Great is our Lord and mighty in power; his understanding has no limit. (Psalm 147:5)

God is greater than our hearts, and he knows everything. (1 John 3:20)

The implications of this are huge. Just like my children find comfort by looking to me when they don't know what's going on, we can do the same. We can find comfort when we look to God who already knows everything.

I heard an amazing interview with NFL coach Sherman Smith recently. He was telling a story about one of his football players who'd had a devastating injury on the field. The player's reaction was stunning. Facing the end of his football career, he said, "I'm excited! Because as a Christian, nothing happens in my life that hasn't been filtered through God's hands first."

As a Christian, nothing happens in my life that hasn't been filtered through God's hands first.

What an amazing perspective! When something scary happens to us, God is not up in heaven wringing his hands. He's not pacing around with sweaty palms and a furrowed brow thinking, *Uh-oh, I never saw* this *coming!*

No. Our God knows everything. He knows every thought, feeling, desire, dream, worry, fear, and problem before you have it. He knows every star in the sky and every hair on your head. He knows every minute of every day you've ever had and every one you will have. He knows. *Everything.*

So when the rug is pulled out from beneath you, when you feel like you're hanging on by a thread, or when fear corners you— remember where to look. Look at the face of the one who will smile and comfort you, the one who will embrace you and remind you that it's going to be okay. Because he already knows. He's got this, and most of all, he's got you.

REFLECTION AND PRAYER

How do you feel when you can't control what's going on? What fears creep up when you don't know what the outcome is going to be? How does your perspective change when you remember that the God who loves you already *knows what's going to happen?*

Spend some time in prayer today asking God to help you find confidence in the fact that he already knows everything. Ask him to help you remember that he's got this—and he's got you.

GOD IS
All-Knowing

God Is All-Powerful

"With man this is impossible,
but with God all things are possible."
—MATTHEW 19:26

*M*y friend Lisa Harper is amazing. She's a brilliant Bible teacher and hilarious storyteller. Lisa adopted her daughter, Missy, from Haiti. And several years back, she and Missy decided to return to the village where Missy was born.

During their stay, Lisa hosted a small Bible study to encourage some of the local women. During one of those meet-ups, a lady came up to Lisa frantic, pointing to her knee and talking loudly in Creole. Lisa looked down and was horrified by what she saw. This lady's knee had swollen to the size of a huge grapefruit. It was oozing . . . *something*, and it smelled terrible. The woman was obviously desperate for help, but Lisa had no idea what was going on or what she was supposed to do about it.

Compelled to do *something*, Lisa reached in her bag and pulled out some peppermint oil to rub on the lady's knee. *Well, she thought, this might make it feel tingly so she'll think something is happening and, at the very least, it will make it smell better!*

Lisa put some peppermint oil in her hands and rubbed them together. Then she placed her hands on the lady's knee and began to pray that God would heal her. Her heart and prayers were genuine—but, come on, this needed more than some peppermint oil and prayers!

When Lisa finished praying, she opened her eyes, looked down, and could not believe it. Her hands were placed on a completely normal-sized knee! The lady's knee had shrunk under her very own hands! Lisa jumped up and ran around screaming like a crazy person in complete disbelief.

I can't blame her. I would have too!

But in the very next moment she felt God say, *Lisa, you're screaming in shock because you didn't believe I could do that.*

I can't tell you how many times I've felt like Lisa—completely shocked when God displays his power in my life in tangible, supernatural, inexplicable, and sometimes scary ways.

God has started my car when it was completely dead. He's put the exact amount of money in my bank account that I desperately needed to pay a bill. He's shrunk massive nodules on my thyroid when doctors said they would only grow. God has performed countless miracles in my life in big and small ways, and every time I'm amazed at what he can do.

Our God is a God of infinite power.

Our God is a God of infinite power. Nothing is too hard for him. You may have heard this story from Matthew before:

> *Then he got into the boat and his disciples followed him. Suddenly a furious storm came up on the lake, so that the waves swept over the boat. But Jesus was sleeping. The disciples went and woke him, saying, "Lord, save us! We're going to drown!" He replied, "You of little faith, why are you so afraid?" Then he got up and rebuked the winds and the waves and it was completely calm. The men were amazed and asked, "What kind of man is this? Even the winds and the waves obey him!"* (Matthew 8:23–27)

It's easy to read stories like this and just dismiss them. We think, *Oh, that was just back then. God doesn't do stuff like that now.*

But, friend, *he does.* God not only *can* still show his power in amazing ways, he actually *loves* to. Christine Caine says, "Impossible is where God begins." Even though you and I hate being painted into a corner, God loves it. It's that exact scenario that allows God to show up and display what he can do.

You might need a door to be opened today, a test result to be clear, a marriage to be saved, a car to be started, or a knee to be shrunk. Whatever it is, I want you to know that God *can* do it. Not just "back then" and for "them"—but today, *right now*. And even for you and me.

REFLECTION AND PRAYER

How do you see God working in your circumstances? Where in your life do you need God to show up and perform a miracle?

Spend time in prayer today reading this aloud: "I pray that the eyes of your heart may be enlightened in order that you may know the hope to which he has called you, the riches of his glorious inheritance in his holy people, and his incomparably great power for us who believe" *(Ephesians 1:18–19).*

Spend some time in prayer today asking God to help you see his power at work in your life in a new way. Ask him to perform a miracle where you need it—and ask him to help you really, genuinely believe that he will do it.

GOD IS
All-Powerful

DAY 6

God Is on Time

_____

"For the vision is yet for the appointed time; . . .
Though it tarries, wait for it; For it will certainly come,
it will not delay."
—HABAKKUK 2:3 (NASB)

*I*n my midtwenties, I was pretty lonely. I was living on a forty-acre farm by myself and working crazy hours at my job with no time to see friends or have much of a life. During those years, I was a bridesmaid approximately 497 times, and I constantly wondered about, dreamed about, and *begged* God for when I would be next.

That fall, as weird as it might sound, I started feeling very strongly that God was telling me I was going to meet my husband soon. And wouldn't you know, a few months later when I joined a running group, I met a guy. On paper, this guy was awesome. On paper.

We started dating and I quickly realized that, in real life, he was just about the worst. He didn't have a steady job and, according to him, had no desire to live above the poverty line. He was also pretty awful to me. He didn't pick me up for dates, didn't pay for them, and never even considered buying me flowers, because as he said, he was "not that kind of a guy." He was sort of terrible.

Now, no one has ever accused me of being a pushover. So the fact that I continued to stick around for this guy made no sense to anyone—not to my mom, not to my friends, not even to the guy! But for some reason, even though I wanted to end it, I felt God say to stay. *Just hang on until August, Christy*, I felt him say. *Just hang on until August.*

Fantastic! I thought. *In August, this joker will get a job, start dressing better than a hobo, and actually be nice to me. It will be a wonderful Jesus redemption story, and we'll get married. I just have to hang on until August.*

This went on for seven months, but he never came around. He never got a job, never cleaned up his act, and never started being nice to me. And then one day, I felt God release me from it all. I didn't know if it was some terrible test or wilderness journey, but one day, it was just all over and I ended it. And then I cried and cried.

What a waste, I thought. *I didn't meet my husband. There was no redemption story. I'm back at square one, and all I have to show for it is seven months of heartache.*

But that time wasn't really wasted. In fact, God was up to something I couldn't see at the time. About a week later, I got a phone call from a really nice guy who had been in the same running group. I had never been interested in Nice Guy because I was busy preparing to marry future hobo husband, *obviously.*

Nice Guy asked me to get some ice cream and hang out. As we spent the day together, my eyes were opened to the most amazing man who had been there all along, waiting for me, pursuing me. The day of ice cream was the beginning, and my husband, Matt, and I have been together ever since. I look back now at my seven-month wilderness with Mr. Hobo and can see it was a premarriage boot camp, preparing me for the amazing love story I had no idea God was writing.

Months later, when Matt and I looked back at the calendar to see when it all started for us—we realized it was *August 1.* God had said to hang on until August, and he wasn't a day late.

You need to know that God is always on time. Now, he is rarely early! He will take you to the very cliffhanger edge of your faith, but he *will* show up. He might not show up as fast as you want, and he probably won't show up in the way you think. But God has never been late before, and he's not going to start with you. Wherever you are, whatever you're waiting on, you can rest in the reality that our God is always on time.

You can rest in the reality that our God is always on time.

REFLECTION AND PRAYER

Does it change how you feel about your life when you consider that God is always on time? How does your perspective change when you realize God is not asleep at the wheel but actually working things together for you right this very second?

Spend some time in prayer asking God to give you his perspective on his timing and plans for you. Then ask for the trust and patience to wait for him while he works.

God Is Personal

"I have summoned you by name; you are mine."
—Isaiah 43:1

*R*ight after college, I moved to a cute little house on a cute little road about two miles from work. The house backed up to the Harpeth River and, as someone who *loves* the outdoors, I knew I had to get a canoe.

I didn't have the money for a new canoe, but my mom was good friends with a guy who owned a local canoe shop. I asked her if she would talk to him about my buying a cheap, used one. And then I prayed that somehow God would make it happen.

Mom showed up the next week with the most perfect yellow canoe I'd ever seen. Now granted, it didn't have seats, had some small holes, and was pretty beat up. But I didn't care because it was yellow and adorable and—because the canoe shop couldn't use it anymore—*free!* God brought me a canoe, and I was ecstatic.

After a couple of weeks of patching the holes and installing wooden seats, it was ready to take out. That summer, I had the best time canoeing with friends and my dog. To me, it was the greatest canoe in the world.

One day, after a ride down the river, I got back to my house and was too tired to bring it up the very steep hill to the backyard. I pulled it as high on the bank as I could, flipped it over, and left it overnight. After all, the bank was just behind my house. I wasn't worried about it getting stolen.

The next day, I walked out back and the canoe was nowhere to be found. I was devastated. The canoe I had prayed for, that God had given me, that I had worked on and made memories in was gone. I was heartbroken.

The next summer, I moved to a forty-acre farm a couple of miles away, and the same river surrounded that land on several sides. By this time, I had mourned the loss of my yellow God-canoe and was ready to get another one. Slightly embarrassed, I asked my mom if she could talk to her friend again. I made it clear I was happy to pay for it.

Mom called a few days later and said she was bringing one over. I was sitting on the porch as she turned down the driveway, and I couldn't believe my eyes. Sticking out the back of her Suburban was the tip of a yellow canoe! I ran to the car and as soon as I saw it, tears started streaming down my face. It was *the* yellow canoe, *my* yellow canoe! It had the wooden seats I installed and the patches I made. I was stunned—God brought me back my canoe!

I was obviously dying to know how that happened. My mom said the wife of the canoe shop owner saw the canoe with their company logo on it propped up on someone's front porch. Realizing it had been stolen, she took it back to their shop. When my mom called months later about another canoe, they unknowingly gave it to her again.

This is a great example of how personal God is. There's another beautiful example of this in the book of Mark. A woman who had bled for twelve years approaches Jesus in a large crowd for healing, but he doesn't see her.

> *She came up behind him in the crowd and touched his cloak, because she thought, "If I just touch his clothes, I will be healed." Immediately her bleeding stopped and she felt in her body that she was freed from her suffering. At once Jesus realized that power had gone out from him. He turned around in the crowd and asked, "Who touched my clothes?" "You see the people crowding against you," his disciples answered, "and yet you can ask, 'Who touched me?'" But Jesus kept looking around to see who had done it.* (Mark 5:27–32)

Isn't it amazing that God—cares about one woman in a crowd who touched his robe? He also cares about my yellow canoe and me and you. You're not just another face in the crowd to God. He knows you intimately, speaks to you uniquely, and loves you individually. Our God is personal.

REFLECTION AND PRAYER

When has God met you in a way that was extremely significant to you, but likely meaningless to someone else? What desire, need, or fear have you withheld from God because you don't think it's important enough to him?

Spend some time today in prayer talking to God as if he knows you intimately and loves you personally. Because, friend, he does.

God Is the Truth

"Jesus answered, 'I am the way and the truth and the life. No one comes to the Father except through me.'"
—JOHN 14:6

"*I* want the truth!"

It's the classic line from the movie *A Few Good Men* that we all remember—the one where Tom Cruise is going toe-to-toe with a terrifying Jack Nicholson. And, of course, we all know the next line when Jack Nicholson's character immediately yells back, "You can't handle the truth!"

It's the most memorable scene from the entire movie.

As crazy as it sounds, I think that's kind of how we feel about the truth sometimes. We think we want the truth, but then we worry we can't handle it. *What if it hurts my feelings? What if I don't want to face the truth? What if I still want to do it my way?*

At 2019's Passion Conference, I heard a sermon by Matt Chandler based on the story of the Samaritan woman at the well. I'd heard this story before but never quite like this.

Jesus was on his way to Galilee and passed through a little town in Samaria called Sychar. He was tired and decided to get some water at a well.

> *When a Samaritan woman came to draw water,*
> *Jesus said to her, "Will you give me a drink?" ... The*
> *Samaritan woman said to him, "You are a Jew and I*
> *am a Samaritan woman. How can you ask me for a*
> *drink?" (For Jews do not associate with Samaritans.)*
> (John 4:7–9)

They talk a little bit more, and then Jesus says something that seems plain cruel:

> *He told her, "Go, call your husband and come back."*
> *"I have no husband," she replied. Jesus said to her,*
> *"You are right when you say you have no husband.*
> *The fact is, you have had five husbands, and the man*
> *you now have is not your husband. What you have just*
> *said is quite true." (John 4:16–18)*

Now, this just seems mean. He knows she doesn't have a husband, and he knows the man she's with isn't her husband. Why go there? Jesus could get his drink of water and leave, but he doesn't. He goes straight to the truth and calls out her sin. Seems kind of harsh, don't you think?

Matt Chandler pointed out that this is actually the most loving thing he could do. He loves her too much to let her live in a lie. He loves her too much to let her settle for less than God's best. He loves her too much to let her hide her sin. He loves her too much to not bring out the truth.

I know when God convicts you of a sin, it stings. It hurts. It's embarrassing and you want to defend yourself and then hide. I feel the same way. But if we're willing to lean in and listen to the truth God offers us, we'll not only find healing, we'll also be drawn into a deeper relationship with him. We can trust God because he not only tells us the truth, he *is* the truth we've been searching for.

REFLECTION AND PRAYER

How did you feel reading the passage from John 4?
How do you feel when someone tells you the hard
truth you need to hear? How do you usually react?

Spend some time in prayer today asking God to show you ways you can resist the urge to hide from the hard stuff. Ask God to help you lean in, listen, and look for the truth that will bring you closer to him and to who you're created to be.

God Is Unchanging

---

*"Jesus Christ is the same yesterday
and today and forever."*
—HEBREWS 13:8

I remember the first time I sensed God speaking to me. It wasn't an audible voice, but it was a thought so foreign and so loving that it could only be from God. I was walking from my apartment to my car my senior year at the University of Tennessee. I had just gotten off the phone with someone and I had lied. In general, I think most people agree lying isn't okay, but I really, *really* value honesty. That's why, when I walked to the car that day, I couldn't believe I had just done it. I hated lying and, in that moment, I hated myself.

I remember thinking, *God, I don't know why you put up with me.* And, y'all, as bizarre as it sounds, the very next second, this sentence entered my mind: *I don't "put up" with you. I adore you.* Those words stopped me right there in the middle of the parking lot. I was stunned, partially because I recognized that statement as the voice of God, and partially because I couldn't believe God would respond so lovingly to my messing up.

At a Young Life camp where I became a Christian at age fifteen, I remember learning that God loves us, forgives our sins, and wants a relationship with us. But six years later, when I was still screwing up, I couldn't believe God would still have that same response.

But that's not the only time.

When I acted terribly and repeatedly made poor decisions on a trip to Florida with friends in my twenties, I felt that voice again. I was sitting on the beach crying in humiliation and complete disappointment in myself. I watched a young couple playing with their toddler on the beach in front of me. The toddler fell down, scraped her knee, and started crying, and immediately, her mom and dad whisked her up to comfort her. I felt that gentle whisper as tears streamed down my face: *That's what it's like when you fall, Christy. I'm right there to pick you up.*

Then, just a few months ago, as I spent the entire day sobbing tears of shame, I sensed God right there yet again. That morning at a friend's party, I had taken my eyes off my son Conley, and he had run out into the road. My husband spotted him and got to him just as a car flew by, barely missing him. Later that day, as I was weeping and in physical pain over what could have happened, I felt that gentle whisper in my spirit yet again: *We are a team, Christy. Conley is my son, too, and we work together to take care of him.*

Forgiveness. Grace. Love. Again and again and again. God has had the same response to me a million other times in my life because he is unchanging. He is the same today as he was yesterday, as he was two thousand years ago, as he was when he created the earth, as he will be tomorrow and until the end of time.

Everything you know about God—his *goodness*, his *constant presence*, his *faithfulness*, his *knowledge*, his *power*, his *perfect timing*, how *personal* he is—will stay the same. He will never not be those things. Never. Not ever. Not even once. Not even when you screw up badly. Not even when you ignore him for years or decades. Not even when you do something unthinkable, and you just plain hate yourself.

God doesn't "put up" with you. He *adores* you. That will never change because he will never change. As we continue our forty days together, I want you to know that God is your firm, unshakeable foundation. You can build your life securely on him because he is unchanging.

God doesn't "put up" with you. He adores you.

REFLECTION AND PRAYER

Has there been a time in your life when you felt like God left you or was mad at you? How does it feel to remember that God never changes? What difference does that make in how you see God and see yourself?

Spend some time in prayer today asking God to remind you that his love, grace, and forgiveness are unending. Ask him to help you find comfort and confidence in the fact that he is unchanging.

God Is a Loving Father

"And, 'I will be a Father to you,
and you will be my sons and daughters,'
says the Lord Almighty."
—2 CORINTHIANS 6:18

*C*hris Tomlin has a popular worship song that came out a few years ago about how God is a good father. I remember the first time I heard it and how it stuck with me. The chorus keeps repeating those simple words, and it's so powerful when we think of God this way. As we wrap up this first stage of our journey about who God is, I think one of the most important things we need to know is that God is our loving father.

Louie Giglio points out in his book *Not Forsaken* how often we see God as father in the New Testament:

Jesus repeats it over and over and drives this characteristic of God into our souls. The number one image of God that Jesus draws for us again and again is this: God is a Father.... 189 times in the four Gospels alone, Jesus referred to God as a father, far more than any other term, distinction, or characteristic Jesus used to describe Him.[1]

This might be hard to wrap your head around, especially if your earthly dad hurt you. If your dad was abusive, alcoholic, absent, or altogether awful, it might be hard to imagine God as your father—much less a loving one. It's normal to see and relate to God the way you do your earthly dad. This is only natural since the relationship with our earthly dad is the blueprint for the only father-daughter relationship we've ever known. It's also more tangible and visible than our relationship with our heavenly father.

But I can tell you from experience, from the moment God captured my heart at fifteen to the first time he spoke to me while I was walking through my apartment complex parking lot—and countless times since—God is not intimidated, deterred, or discouraged by our struggle to see him as a loving father. In fact, I believe he's on a mission to make himself known to me and you as our loving father. I think God even wants to redefine fatherhood altogether and show you how he is your perfect father—something no earthly dad could ever measure up to, no matter how great he was or is.

A beautiful picture of this is the story of the Prodigal Son. Jesus told this story in the book of Luke about a man who had two sons. The younger son asked for his inheritance early—something absolutely unheard of in that day. In that culture, it was essentially the son saying to his father: "I wish you were dead." And what did he do with the inheritance when he received it? He left home to *"squander his wealth in wild living"* (Luke 15:13). He spent every last dime, and soon after, there was a famine. After struggling to survive, he realized he should go back to his dad and ask to be his servant in order to have enough to eat and stay alive. Embarrassed, dirty, starving, and with his head hung in shame, he went home. And the Bible says,

> *But while he was still a long way off, his father saw*
> *him and was filled with compassion for him; he ran to*
> *his son, threw his arms around him and kissed him. . . .*
> *The father said to his servants, "Quick! Bring the*
> *best robe and put it on him. Put a ring on his finger*
> *and sandals on his feet. Bring the fattened calf and*
> *kill it. Let's have a feast and celebrate. For this son of*
> *mine was dead and is alive again; he was lost and is*
> *found."* (Luke 15:20–24)

What a beautiful story about how God feels about us as our loving father! Even when we offend him and mess up, he's filled with compassion for us. He runs to us. He throws his arms around us and kisses us. He doesn't cast the stones of condemnation we deserve, but instead, celebrates us. Like Chris Tomlin says, he really is a good, good *father*.

REFLECTION AND PRAYER

What do you feel when you think of God as a father? Do you find yourself interacting with God like you do your earthly dad? Think of a time when God has shown you that he's your father who adores you.

Spend some time in prayer today asking God to show you how he is not just your father—but a perfect father.

SECTION
TWO

Who You Are

I've gone through quite a few phases in my life—some of which were . . . *interesting*.

I took Latin and ballroom dance lessons for two years after college. I even competed in a dance competition in the rumba, cha-cha, and swing categories. I did the farm thing, complete with horses, barn cats, a mini-donkey, and two fainting goats: Willie and Waylon. (The fainting goats served no practical purpose on the farm, by the way. I bought them purely for my entertainment because it was funny when they passed out for no reason.) I went through a pretty strong pop phase in college when I wore bedazzled do-rags trying to be like J.Lo. And one time in my twenties, I played for two years on an adult soccer team with all Guatemalan men that spoke exactly zero English.

I've been sporty, country, pop, and everything in between.

With each of these . . . *experiments*, what I was really trying to do was find myself. What did I love? What reflected my personality, values, and identity? Who was I? But when I got a full-time job that I love and got married and had kids, all of that changed. I didn't have to find myself anymore because it was all predetermined for me with the roles and titles that came with those life changes. I am Matt's wife. I am Carter, Conley, and soon to be Mary Grace's mom. I am a speaker, author, and business coach. That's me.

It's easy to do, isn't it? We look to others to tell us who we are. We define ourselves in response to the people and world around us. The only problem is that you and I are so much more than that. You were more before those roles became a part of your life, and you are more while you have those titles, and you are more even if or when those labels change. It's that "more" that we're going to explore in section 2. Because now that we have a more accurate picture of who God is, we're going to see what God has to say about who *you* are.

YOU ARE
More

You Were Created

"For you created my inmost being;
you knit me together in my mother's womb."
—Psalm 139:13

I have this theory that when some people are around a pregnant person, they become socially stupid. They aren't stupid people. But the moment they're in the presence of a woman who's expecting, it's as if all logic, intelligence, empathy, and social skills go completely out the window.

"Wow! You're HUGE!"

"Are you sure there aren't two in there?"

"You're about to POP!"

First of all, for the record, babies don't just "pop" out. Second of all, in what universe is it *ever* okay to tell a woman she's "huge" or make a statement that she looks like she has an *entire additional human* in her belly that's not there? People can be crazy. I love them, but they can be crazy.

One of the many personal things people have asked me during this third pregnancy is the fun and slightly awkward question: "Oh wow . . . so was this *planned*?" I'm a pretty lighthearted person, so I roll with this question. But it makes me think of something that's important for us to remember.

Regardless of how people plan their families, I want to remind you that God planned you. Long before your mom and dad ever met or were even born, God thought of you first. You were his idea. And most importantly, as we begin to explore all of the things that make you who you are, I want to remind you that he created you.

God planned you.

Psalm 139:13–16 says:

> *For you created my inmost being;*
> *you knit me together in my mother's womb.*
> *I praise you because I am fearfully and wonderfully*
> *   made;*
> *your works are wonderful,*
> *I know that full well.*
> *My frame was not hidden from you*

when I was made in the secret place,
when I was woven together in the depths of the earth.
Your eyes saw my unformed body
all the days ordained for me were written in your book
before one of them came to be.

I love this picture of creation. Of all of the things we can look to in order to find our identity, it's important to start here. God not only created the heavens and the earth, the stars in the sky, the birds in the air, and the fish in the sea, he also created you and me. He created every hair on your head, every freckle, and every perfectly unique fingerprint. He didn't just create your physical body, though. He also created your mind, your personality, your desires, dreams, gifts, talents, and strengths. He created everything about you that makes you *you*. You are his creation.

I was reminded of this one day when I was going for a trail run on a beautiful Sunday afternoon. I was overcome with how beautiful the nature around me was. I've always seen and felt God in nature, but this day was particularly beautiful. The sun was shining, the leaves on the trees were glistening, and the breeze was blowing gently. The only things I could hear were the sounds of the dirt crunching beneath my shoes, my heart pounding, and my strained breathing with each step I took. I felt so close to God and so alive in that moment.

As I ran, I thought, *God, I just love enjoying your creation*. And I felt that familiar whisper immediately respond, *I love enjoying my creation enjoying my creation*.

Oh, wow. He was talking about *me*. I am also his creation and he enjoys me.

It's an incredible identity shift when you remember you're God's beautiful creation. So when you're feeling like a failure or fraud or just flawed, remember that God made you and he doesn't make mistakes. He created you on purpose and with a purpose. God didn't need anything else in the world, and yet he thought of you. He wanted you, he planned you, and he created you. And he doesn't just love you, he also likes you and even enjoys you.

REFLECTION AND PRAYER

Go back and read Psalm 139:13–16 aloud. (Really do it!) Let those words and that truth sink into your mind and spirit. God created you. You were wonderfully made. *How does that make you feel? Does it change how you view yourself when you remember that you are God's beautiful creation?*

Spend some time in prayer today asking God to help you remember that you were always a part of his perfect plan. Ask him to help you see yourself how he sees you—as his beautiful creation who he loves, likes, and even enjoys.

You Were Created with a Powerful Mind

"We demolish arguments and every pretension that sets itself up against the knowledge of God, and we take captive every thought to make it obedient to Christ."
—2 CORINTHIANS 10:5

I was enjoying something I *never* get these days: alone time. I had a day off of work and decided to have a little getaway for myself and head to a lake in Alabama.

I got down there that night and decided to finally finish a little project hemming curtains. I switched on all the lights in the house, set up my sewing machine on the small kitchen table, and turned on *The Greatest Showman.* I was really in a groove and loving life when out of nowhere, the power went out.

I went from having forty-seven lights on with a musical blaring and sewing machine humming to complete silence, sitting in darkness so dark I couldn't see my hand in front of my face. I was in the middle of nowhere country, and I don't think I'd ever experienced anything that dark in my life.

And in that moment, I knew exactly what had happened.

The killer was outside.

He had cut the power, just like in scary movies, and now he was coming to get me. My heart started to race, my palms got sweaty, and I could barely breathe. I fumbled around the pitch-black darkness to find my phone and turn on the flashlight. My battery was at 17 percent. I started lighting every candle I could find. My heart was pounding so hard in my chest that it physically hurt. I realized I needed a weapon to defend myself against the killer and grabbed the largest butcher knife I could find.

It was at this moment—when I was alone in the middle of the pitch-black night, wide-eyed and wild-haired, holding a butcher knife and surrounded by five hundred lit candles like a weird séance—that I realized something: The terrifying person in this scenario was *me*!

I quickly pushed that thought aside, though, because as everyone knows, this is the point in the scary movie when you're screaming at the girl on the screen: "You have to get out of there! He's coming! *Run!*" So that's exactly what I did. I blew out the candles as fast as I could, grabbed my car keys, and ran—phone flashlight in one hand and butcher knife in the other—all the way to my car. I started the ignition and headed straight home.

I acted out of the story I *believed*.

It turns out it was storms, and not a mass murderer, that knocked the power out. But that doesn't matter because that's not what I believed. I acted out of the story my mind believed. I don't know about you, but that's one of the many times my mind has run away with me.

Part of what makes you *you* is your mind. God created us with incredibly powerful minds. Like the lake house example, we will experience what we believe in our minds—so we need to be very careful to control our thoughts.

We are in control of our thoughts.

Second Corinthians 10:4–5 reminds us that we are in control of our thoughts:

We take captive every thought to make it obedient to Christ.

Philippians 4:8 tells us what to think about:

Whatever is true, whatever is noble, whatever is right, whatever is pure, whatever is lovely, whatever is

*admirable—if anything is excellent or praiseworthy—
think about such things.*

Romans 12:2 tells us to renew our minds in order to transform our lives:

*Do not conform to the pattern of this world, but be
transformed by the renewing of your mind.*

These are choices we make and actions we take. What you put into your mind, what you allow to stay there, and what you focus on are all up to you. Proverbs 4:23 says, *"Be careful what you think, because your thoughts run your life"* (NCV). God created you with a mind that has incredible power to control not only your actions, but also how you experience your circumstances. And what you do with it is up to you.

REFLECTION AND PRAYER

*What types of things do you find yourself thinking
about or focusing on during the day? Take
inventory of your mental input one day. Are the
relationships, entertainment, experiences, social
media, and other sources of influence helping
the renewing of your mind or hurting it?*

Spend some time in prayer today asking God to show you ways you can start renewing the powerful mind he has given you in order to transform your life.

YOU WERE CREATED WITH A

Powerful Mind

You Were Created Unique

---

*"But in fact God has placed the parts in the body,
every one of them,
just as he wanted them to be."*
—1 CORINTHIANS 12:18

*A*re you into the Enneagram? You can always tell who is because . . . well, they'll tell you. I remember when the Enneagram started becoming more popular a few years ago, and it seemed like everyone was talking about it.

"Oh, she's a 3 wing 4. So typical."
"She's a 9 but she's leaning in to her 1 wing right now."
"Well, he *is* a 5 wing 6 so *you know . . .*"

No, I don't know! Well, I didn't at the time anyway. Until I became one of them.

So, what's the Enneagram anyway? According to Ian Cron's definition in *The Road Back to You*, it's "an ancient personality typing system. It helps people understand who they are and what makes them tick."[2] And whether we take a Myers-Briggs assessment, read *StrengthsFinder*, use the DiSC, or some other personality system, they all point to the same truth: All of us were created uniquely.

It might be tempting to see someone with different strengths than you have and wish you were more like them. But if you were like them, you wouldn't be you. God created you to be like you—because he wants *you* in the world.

It can also be tempting to see someone with different qualities than you have—maybe qualities that get on your nerves—and think about how wrong they are. You would never do things that way! And instead of looking up to them, wishing you were more like that, you feel a pull toward pride, judging them for being the way they are. But you know what? God created them too—because he needs them in the world also.

I love how 1 Corinthians 12:14–19 says,

Even so the body is not made up of one part but of many. Now if the foot should say, "Because I am not a hand, I do not belong to the body," it would not for that reason stop being part of the body. And if the ear should say, "Because I am not an eye, I do not belong to the body," it would not for that reason stop being part of the body. If the whole body were an eye, where would the sense of hearing be? If the whole body were an ear, where would the sense of smell be? But in fact God has placed the parts in the body, every one of them, just as he wanted them to be.

Just like our physical body needs ears and eyes, hands and feet, the world needs you and me and all of the things that make us each unique. It needs extroverts and introverts, loud people and quiet people, passionate people and easygoing people. The world needs what you have to offer, just as you are, just as you were created. God wants to show himself to the world through you in a way that's unique to you. No one can do what you can do like you can do it.

So if you struggle with wishing you were more like someone else or if you struggle with judging others, let 1 Corinthians 12 encourage you. God created you uniquely, and he has a plan for all of those amazing attributes he gave you. There's a reason you're wired the way you are, and there's a reason everyone else is wired the way they are. The world needs all of us—with every personality, preference, tendency, and tick. And together, we all make up the body of Christ.

REFLECTION AND PRAYER

Do you tend to think of your way as the "right" way, or do you wish you were different and more like someone else? How does it change your perspective when you consider God created you that way for a reason?

Spend some time in prayer today asking God to give you an appreciation not only for your own unique attributes, but also for the unique qualities of others who are different from you.

You Were Created with Talents and Gifts

"Let your light shine."
—MATTHEW 5:16

---

*J*ackson was the *best* dog. He was this huge, beautiful, loving Bernese Mountain Dog, and I got him my senior year of college. My aunt and I drove eleven and a half hours to Oklahoma to get him because there weren't any in Tennessee. He was my companion dog and went with me everywhere. He was with me through countless moves, boyfriends, breakups, roommate changes, and a million life transitions. He was my baby before I had actual babies.

Several years ago, back when Jackson was still alive, I was with my in-laws celebrating my birthday. We were sitting at our kitchen table and had just finished eating dinner. They gave me a coffee mug and a candle, and then my mother-in-law handed me a large square package. She seemed to save it for last, so I knew it must be special. I tore off the wrapping paper and it was a framed image of a Bernese Mountain Dog. I thought, *Well, that is so nice. Bernese Mountain Dogs are pretty rare, so it's not like you can just find art or key chains or bumper stickers of them at the store. She must have had to search a long time or special order this.* I thanked her for the gift and set it to the side. I thought there was probably an empty space in the upstairs hallway where I could hang it.

We finished dinner, cleaned up, and I told my in-laws goodbye as they headed back to their home in Alabama. After they left, my husband said, "Babe, I don't know if you knew this, but Mom didn't *buy* that for you. She drew it. That's not just any Bernese Mountain Dog. That's Jackson."

I was speechless. Do you know how differently I viewed that gift once I knew that? Do you know how much more I appreciated that gift? How much more I *treasured* that gift? I wanted to put it on display in the center of my house for everyone to see when I realized it wasn't some random product rolled off an assembly line for the masses—but created for me by someone who loved me very much.

Friend, how differently would you look at your own gifts—how much more would you treasure them and want to put them on display for everyone to see—if you knew they were not randomly rolled off an assembly line, but created for you by a God who loves you very much?

---

*Your gifts were created for you by a
God who loves you very much.*

God didn't just create your mind and your personality, he created your gifts, talents, and passions. The things you love to do that make you light up? That's not a coincidence. The things that make you come alive? That's not an accident. God gave you those gifts when he created you, so don't hide them in some back hallway of your life.

Matthew 5:14–16 says:

*You are the light of the world. A town built on a hill
cannot be hidden. Neither do people light a lamp and
put it under a bowl. Instead they put it on its stand,
and it gives light to everyone in the house. In the same
way, let your light shine before others, that they may
see your good deeds and glorify your Father in heaven.*

Do you understand what these verses are saying? When you shine in your talents, people see God. So shine, friend. Don't hold back in the name of being humble. You're not doing anyone any favors by dismissing or downplaying your strengths because you think it's selfish. God made you good at things—so own them. And more than that, step into them. I promise you, the world needs what you have to offer. They need to see God in a way that only you can show them. Don't hide your lamp under a bowl—the world needs to see God. The world needs you to let your light shine.

REFLECTION AND PRAYER

What are you good at? Make a list of the talents God has given you—they can be anything from painting to patience and organizing to origami. There's no right or wrong answer here, just write it all down, even if it makes you uncomfortable. These talents are a gift from God. And they're not only for you to enjoy, but also for you to bless others with.

Spend some time in prayer today asking God to show you what talents and gifts he gave you, and ask him to show you more opportunities to use them. Ask him to help you see your gifts as something to be appreciated, treasured, and displayed—and to help you let your light shine so others can see more of him.

You Were Created with God-Given Desires

"Delight yourself in the LORD, and he will give you the desires of your heart."
—Psalm 37:4 (ESV)

I had always wanted to live on a farm from as far back as I could remember. So when I got the opportunity to rent a house on forty acres at the age of twenty-three, I jumped on it. Nevermind the fact that I was single, working eighty hours a week for an entry-level salary, and had absolutely zero experience on a farm. I thought I'd go for it and just figure it out when I got there. After all, this had been a lifelong dream of mine.

What I didn't realize at the time, but figured out soon after, is that the reality of farm life was quite different than the dream in my head. I had imagined sitting on the front porch of the old farmhouse sipping sweet tea, listening to the birds chirp, and watching the horses graze in the field.

Instead, my days started at 4:00 a.m. by putting on my muck boots and trucking out to the barn to break up the ice in the trough so the horses could drink. I mucked the stalls, hauled the hay, bushhogged the fields, fixed the barbed wire fences, and oh by the way, fed and cared for all the animals every day. By myself. At twenty-three. While working eighty hours a week in my real job that was burning me out a little more each day.

After about a year of "living the dream," I was exhausted. I was thankful for the experience, but I knew I needed something new. One day I was standing on my deck, worn down from my day job and farm life, and I felt stuck. So I prayed, *God, I don't think I'll ever find a company I believe in as much as the YMCA. I love that we change lives.* And as crazy as it sounds, I felt these words enter my mind instantly: *You're going to work for Dave Ramsey.*

I thought, *Great! . . . Who's Dave Ramsey?*

My laptop was open on the table near me, so I walked over and searched "Dave Ramsey." The first result said, "Based in Nashville, Tennessee." *Fantastic!* I thought. *I don't even have to move to a new city!*

That moment changed my life forever.

I'd never had the dream or desire to work for Ramsey Solutions. I didn't even know who Dave Ramsey was! But that's why I love Psalm 37:4: *"Delight yourself in the LORD, and he will give you the desires of your heart."* That doesn't mean he's a genie in a bottle and you always get what you want. It means that as you lean into him and his plans for you, he will show you what your desires are. He might not put the words directly into your mind, but he will open a door, give you an idea, stir something in your heart, or maybe just gently remind you of a dream you've forgotten. But he doesn't stop there. After God shows you what your desires are, he loves to fulfill them.

After God spoke a new dream to me that day, I took action on it and was amazed as he fulfilled every detail from applying to getting hired to finding a little house to rent close to the office. He even showed me a plan for all of my animals. I donated them to a Young Life camp in North Carolina where I had worked in college. My animals are still all together making high school kids happy. God didn't miss a single step in providing for the new desire he'd given me.

God loves to not only show you new desires, but he also wants to draw out ones you've had for a long time. For example, when people came to Jesus for a miracle, he often asked them the same question: "What do you want me to do for you?"

When two blind men called out to Jesus from the roadside,

Jesus stopped and called them. "What do you want me to do for you?" he asked. "Lord," they answered, "we want our sight." (Matthew 20:32–33)

He knew, of course! He asked this question for their benefit, not his.

God wants to draw out your desires and then he wants you to trust him with the fulfillment of them. So what do you want God to do for you? Delight yourself in him and watch what he'll do!

REFLECTION AND PRAYER

How do you feel about your dreams and desires?
How does it feel to think that God wants to
draw out your desires and fulfill them?

Spend some time in prayer today asking God
to show you what your dreams are and for the
patience and faith to trust him to fulfill them.

You Were Created with an Amazing Body

"Do you not know that your bodies are temples of the Holy Spirit, who is in you, whom you have received from God? You are not your own; you were bought at a price. Therefore honor God with your bodies."

—1 CORINTHIANS 6:19–20

*M*y advertising professor shared a story during my senior year that has stuck with me my entire life. The semester before, she had asked her class to research and write a report on an advertisement that promoted something not real or achievable.

One of the young women in her class just so happened to be a Calvin Klein underwear model in Milan. For her report, she turned in a page from a glossy magazine where her flawless body was featured on a full-page advertisement wearing a Calvin Klein bra and underwear. She had circled every single part of her body that had been photoshopped and "corrected." She included only one sentence: "So even I can't be me."

Even a Calvin Klein underwear model—arguably a gold standard of body perfection and beauty—wasn't good enough.

Statistics show that 91 percent of women are unhappy with their bodies.[3] Ninety-one.

Let's say that another way:

- Ninety-one percent of women don't like the way they look or feel.
- Ninety-one percent of women don't like the body God created for them.
- Ninety-one percent of women don't like this prominent and very visible part of who they are.

I get it. I'm in that 91 percent too. I've got scars and stretch marks and wrinkles and creases and gray hair and at least thirty other "problems" I'm too embarrassed to admit publicly. It's insanely difficult not to focus on all of the things we don't like about ourselves when we're constantly bombarded with an impossible standard of beauty.

But did you know that despite the infinite list of complaints about this body God has given us, our bodies are actually amazing? I don't mean "amazing" in the sense that you can just snap your fingers and instantly love your loose skin or wrinkles. Your body is amazing because of what it can do. Here are some examples:

1. The human nose can detect one trillion smells.[4]
2. Human eyes are the equivalent of a 576 megapixel digital camera.[5] (For comparison, the most expensive digital camera in the world is only about 200 megapixels.)
3. Your bones are roughly five times stronger than steel.[6]

Our bodies are more intelligent than any computer and more complex than any machine. And even more than that, the Bible tells us our bodies are a temple of the Holy Spirit. Think about it: The Spirit resides in this body that 91 percent of us hate and complain and talk bad about daily. Your body is literally a temple of the living God. And by the way, you only get one of them in this lifetime.

Like we talked about on Day 11, God *created* our bodies. He gave them to us. He actually loves your body, and I'd be willing to bet he wants you to love it as well. So before we go on bashing our body from morning to night, focusing on every seeming imperfection, let's make an effort to realize our bodies are an incredible gift from God.

He actually loves your body, and I'd be willing to bet he wants you to love it as well.

"Honor God with your bodies" (1 Corinthians 6:20). But don't just honor it by what you eat and drink, or by going to the doctor. Don't just honor it with exercise and staying away from things that damage it. Honor your body in how you look at it, think about it, and talk about it. Brené Brown says, "Talk to yourself like you would someone you love." Your body—whether you like it or not—is a gift from God and a huge part of who you are. And if you're going to get back to yourself and who you were created to be, I guarantee you that choosing to love your amazing body is a very important step in that journey.

REFLECTION AND PRAYER

What are some things you love about your body? What has it done that amazes you? Is it hard to focus on those things? Why or why not? How does it change your perspective when you think of your body as a gift God gave you and as the temple of the Holy Spirit?

Spend some time in prayer today confessing any ways you've mistreated your body (even if only in your thoughts). Ask God for help seeing your body the way he does.

You Were Chosen

---

*"You did not choose Me but I chose you, and
appointed you that you would go and bear fruit, and
that your fruit would remain, so that whatever you ask
of the Father in My name He may give to you."*
—John 15:16 (NASB)

*M*y favorite thing to play growing up was kickball. Whether we were playing during middle school recess or in someone's backyard on the weekend, I loved the game. However, getting ready to play also stirred up a tormenting fear I had: *Please, please, please don't let me get picked last!*

It's the worst feeling, isn't it? Whether it's for a kickball team, a class project in college, or just grouping up in a team-building activity at work or church, everyone has this deep-seated fear of not being chosen. It's the feeling of walking into the school lunch-room with a tray in your hands, your eyes scanning the cafeteria looking for a familiar face, a spot to sit, a place to belong.

We all have this deep need to be chosen.

The good news is: *We already are.* You are chosen by the God of the universe. He had a choice, and he saw you and thought, *Look at her! I want that one. She's mine.*

I love how the story of Esther in the Bible illustrates this.

Esther was a Jewish orphan, raised by her cousin Mordecai when her father and mother died. When King Xerxes put out a year-long search for a new queen, Esther was among the many women pampered and prepped to be considered. Esther didn't reveal her Jewish background during this process, likely because it could have disqualified her or even put her in danger due to the strong anti-Jewish sentiment in the palace. Despite the many women the king saw, he chose Esther to be queen. But that's not even the amazing part of the story. The really cool part is that God was choosing Esther to save her people—she just didn't know it yet.

While she was queen, Esther's Uncle Mordecai made the king's new adviser so angry he wanted Mordecai and all of the Jewish people killed to pay for the offense. Mordecai was devastated and terrified. He sent a message to Esther pleading with her to *"go into the king's presence to beg for mercy and plead with him for her people"* (Esther 4:8).

The only problem was there was a law that you would be put to death for going to the king without being summoned—even if you were the queen. Esther hadn't been summoned by the king and didn't know what to do. Mordecai pressed on with one of the most famous verses from the entire book of Esther:

> *If you keep quiet at a time like this, deliverance and relief for the Jews will arise from some other place, but you and your relatives will die. Who knows if perhaps you were made queen for just such a time as this?* (Esther 4:14 NLT)

Esther rises to the challenge, risks her life, and boldly goes before the king. She saves the entire Jewish people and becomes a hero. She was chosen. Chosen by the king to be his queen. Chosen by Mordecai to help her people. Chosen by God for such a time as this.

And so were you. You have been chosen. God chose you for a relationship with him. He chose you for the family you have, the life that you lead, and the plans he has for you—plans you may not even know yet. This means you don't have to worry about being picked last on the kickball team or not having a seat at the lunchroom table. You don't have to live in fear of being left out because you've already been chosen by a God who loves you very much.

REFLECTION AND PRAYER

*What fears do you have about being rejected?
Have you ever had an experience where you
were picked last and left out? How did that make
you feel? How does it change your perspective
about your value and worth to God when you
realize he hud a choice and he chose you?*

*Spend some time in prayer today asking God to
show you what it means to live as his chosen child.*

You Are Able

---

*"I pray that the eyes of your heart may be enlightened
in order that you may know the hope to which he has
called you, the riches of his glorious inheritance in his
holy people, and his incomparably great power for us
who believe."*

—EPHESIANS 1:18–19

We had never done anything like this before. It was a new brand, new event, new message, and new audience—and a completely new role for me at work. It was October of 2015, and our very first Business Boutique event was just a few weeks away. I was freaking out. I remember sitting in this exact same home office I'm sitting in now, crying hysterically. I was having a complete meltdown from the pressure I felt to pull off this massive project. I had been working tirelessly on every aspect of this three-day event: from the sessions to the slides, the workbook to the stage notes, and everything in between. I just kept thinking, *I can't do this. They've got this all wrong. I am not the girl for this. I don't know what to teach. I don't know what to say. I can't do this!*

In a moment of desperation, I grabbed my Bible, and it fell open to Exodus 3 and 4 where God is asking Moses to rescue the Israelites from captivity in Egypt. After God gives Moses his instructions—what to do, where to go, what to say—Moses starts to waver. He questions and doubts. God appears in a burning bush and then, as a sign, turns Moses's staff into a snake and back to a staff again—but Moses still isn't convinced. The call is too big. The ask is too much. He feels unqualified. He doesn't think he can do it.

Sound familiar? We've all been there. Many times.

Moses tries to reason with God: *"Pardon your servant, Lord. I have never been eloquent, neither in the past nor since you have spoken to your servant. I am slow of speech and tongue"* (Exodus 4:10).

And God replied, "Oh, right! I totally forgot about that! I'll ask someone else I created with more refined public speaking skills. Sorry to bug you, Moses."

Does that sound right? Of course not. In my own personal freak-out that day in my home office, I read God's actual response:

The LORD said to him, "Who gave human beings their mouths? Who makes them deaf or mute? Who

gives them sight or makes them blind? Is it not I, the
LORD? Now go; I will help you speak and will teach
you what to say." (Exodus 4:11–12)

God was speaking directly to me through his Word in that moment. And then I sensed his gentle, familiar voice say, *Christy, you are freaking out because you think this is your event. This is not your event. This is my event, and I will be the one to pull it off.*

Anything is possible if a person believes. (Mark 9:23 NLT)

It's so easy to do. We look at our own imperfections and limitations, and we're overwhelmed with the task in front of us—the task we mistakenly think is ours to complete. Of course we're overwhelmed! In our own strength, we can't do much. But Scripture says, *"I can do all things through Christ who strengthens me"* (Philippians 4:13 NKJV). Not just some things. Not just easy things. Not just things I can figure out and manipulate and control myself. No—*all* things. Anything.

Anything is possible if a person believes.
(Mark 9:23 NLT)

The same Spirit who empowered Jesus and who parted the Red Sea before Moses lives in you and me. *You are able*—and not if you just work a little harder. Not if you just get a little smarter. Not if you just had a little more money, time, or skills. You are able right now.

Bestselling author Mark Batterson says, "God doesn't call the qualified. He qualifies the called." As you get back to you, know that you are able to do anything and everything God has in store for you because the all-powerful God we talked about on Day 5 lives in you.

The one who calls you is faithful, and he will do it.
(1 Thessalonians 5:24)

REFLECTION AND PRAYER

When God asks you to do something that feels too big to handle, do you remind him why you can't? Read Exodus 4:11–12 again. How does it change your perspective when you remember that the one who's calling you is the one who will give you the power to do it?

Spend some time in prayer today asking God to help you remember that you're able and can do

all things *through Christ who strengthens you.
Ask him to give you an opportunity to showcase
his power in you, and then ask him for the courage
and strength to step out in faith and do it.*

YOU ARE
Able

You Are Responsible

"A man reaps what he sows."
—GALATIANS 6:7

*D*ave Ramsey tells a story about a man who was traveling through a small town. The man was walking along the road when he passed a beautiful farm. The traveler stopped to admire its beauty. The fields and crops were perfect, the white fence was pristine, the landscaping around the house was immaculate, and the house was flawless. The whole scene looked like something out of a postcard. The traveler saw the old farmer working in the field in his dirty overalls and called out to him: "Farmer, this place is beautiful! God has really blessed you!"

And the old farmer replied, "Yes, sir, he has. And you should have seen what this place looked like when God had it all to himself."

I love that story because it not only illustrates God's blessings in our lives, but also the responsibility we have as well. We aren't just passive puppets, waiting for God to orchestrate everything. We are active participants and partners with God. We are responsible for the choices we make and the actions we take. It's not "all God," and it's not "all us." It's both. We live in a cause-and-effect world and, good or bad, we will reap what we sow.

Jesus teaches about this in the Parable of the Talents.

It will be like a man going on a journey, who called his servants and entrusted his wealth to them. To one he gave five bags of gold, to another two bags, and to another one bag, each according to his ability. Then he went on his journey. The man who had received five bags of gold went at once and put his money to work and gained five bags more. So also, the one with two bags of gold gained two more. But the man who had received one bag went off, dug a hole in the ground and hid his master's money. (Matthew 25:14–18)

Each of the men made choices in how they managed their gold. And after a time, the master returned to settle accounts. The man with five bags of gold and the man with two bags showed the master they had each doubled what they had received. The master replied to both,

> *Well done, good and faithful servant! You have been*
> *faithful with a few things; I will put you in charge of*
> *many things. Come and share your master's happi-*
> *ness!* (Matthew 25:21)

The man with one bag of gold presented his lone bag back to the master, and his master replied,

> *You wicked, lazy servant! . . . Take the bag of gold*
> *from him and give it to the one who has ten bags. For*
> *whoever has will be given more, and they will have an*
> *abundance. Whoever does not have, even what they*
> *have will be taken from them.* (Matthew 25:26–29)

We have a responsibility to be wise with what we've been given, regardless of the size or amount. That includes everything from our money to our house to our kids and our spouse. It includes our body, work, and time. The Bible reminds us that *"every good and perfect gift is from above"* (James 1:17) and that *"a man reaps what he sows"* (Galatians 6:7). It's both/and. It's us *and* God.

Even when Jesus performed miracles, he gave instructions to those being healed. They had a responsibility in the matter. In John 5:8, to the sick man waiting by the pool for thirty-eight years to be healed, Jesus said, *"Rise, take up your bed and walk"* (NKJV).

To the adulterous woman who was to be stoned in John 8:11, Jesus had mercy on her, saved her, and then said, *"Go and sin no more"* (NKJV).

To the disciples whose feet he was washing in John 13:14, Jesus said, *"You should also wash one another's feet."*

We have a responsibility in this life. Jesus can heal you, but it's up to you to take up your bed and walk. Jesus can save you, but it's up to you to make better choices. Jesus can love and serve you, but it's up to you to love and serve others. You are responsible for your life—no one else. You've got to work like it all depends on you and pray like it all depends on God. I guarantee you're going to need both.

REFLECTION AND PRAYER

Do you ever feel helpless, waiting on God to change your circumstances? Reflect on the tale of the traveler and farmer. How does it resonate with you as you consider that it's both you and God working together to make things happen in your life?

Spend some time in prayer today asking God to help you take responsibility for and manage what he's given you well.

You Are Loved

---

*"See how very much our Father loves us, for he calls us
his children, and that is what we are!"*
—1 JOHN 3:1 (NLT)

*S*everal years ago, when my dad was visiting from out of town, he made an observation about my dog, Jackson: "You can sure tell that dog knows he's loved." Isn't that interesting? He didn't say, "That dog is so loving." He said, "He knows he's loved."

What's so beautiful about my dad's observation is that it's true for all of us. What we offer others is a mirror into what we believe about ourselves. If we want to love others, we have to believe we are loved. *"We love because he first loved us"* (1 John 4:19). After all, we can't offer something we don't have.

As we wrap up exploring who we are and what God says about us, there's no better way than to reset and refocus on the fact that, above all else, we are loved. On Day 10, I mentioned a worship song performed by Chris Tomlin that's really special to me. In addition to talking about how God is a good father, the chorus also says:

"And I'm loved by you
It's who I am, it's who I am, it's who I am . . ."

What if that was it? What if that one line summarizes the most important thing you need to know as you get back to you? You are loved by God—*that* is who you are. That's the source of your identity. That's your value, significance, and worth—and everything else about you pales in comparison. When you know you're loved and truly live from that truth, it changes everything. It changes how you view yourself, how you live your life, how you love others, and even how you recognize God.

I have a million stories about my dog, Jackson, but I'll never forget one particular night at the farm. My friend and I decided to have a fall party and invited a bunch of people over. At one point, we were outside in the fenced-in, medium-sized field between my front yard and the barn. I never let Jackson in this field because he only wanted to chase the animals. The same thing happened every time: He would first race after the fainting goats. They would faint and fall over, and he would proceed to greet them the way all dogs greet each other (by sniffing their privates). The goats didn't really appreciate that invasion of privacy in their paralyzed state on the ground. Then he would chase the mini-donkey, Hank, and the barn cats all over kingdom come. It was complete chaos.

Well, somehow that night, someone at the party accidentally opened the gate where Jackson was eagerly waiting, and he got into the field. Within seconds, complete pandemonium erupted. Jackson sprinted at full speed after all the animals. The animals scattered in every direction. And every single person at the party screamed Jackson's name, trying to get him to stop and come back to the front yard. I knew I had to get him back, but I also knew there was no way he was going to hear me over all the shouting and frantic animal madness. I felt helpless and didn't know what to do. And then I did something that made absolutely no sense in that moment of insanity.

I didn't run after him and I didn't scream. I just stood right in the middle of the field, and in a completely normal tone and volume, said his name one time: "Jackson."

The most amazing thing happened. He froze. He went from full-on sprinting, with animals running in all directions and people yelling from every angle, to a complete statue. He turned toward my voice and walked directly up to me. Why? Because he knew my voice. In the midst of sheer chaos and tons of other voices yelling, he knew *my* voice—the voice of the one who loved him.

The same is true for you and me. When you know you're loved by God, you can discern his voice among all the others in your life. Then, you can find your identity, your source of confidence, and even your sense of peace. Everything changes when you remember that, first and foremost, you are loved by God. God is a good father, and you are loved by him. *That* is who you are.

REFLECTION AND PRAYER

What's it like to think of your main source of identity as simply being loved by God? When you remember that, how does it change your confidence, your sense of purpose, and even the voice you listen to?

Spend some time in prayer today asking God to help you learn to not only remember his love for you, but to actually feel it, even in the midst of chaos in your life.

Where You Are

One of the best parts of living in Nashville is that you get to experience all four seasons. Fall is my favorite, but what I really love is the variety and getting to experience all of them. In the summer, we spend every weekend at the lake on a boat, grilling out and swimming. In the fall, we watch football, go on hikes and hayrides, and visit every pumpkin patch we can find. In the winter, we play in the snow, drink hot chocolate, and enjoy the fireplace. In the spring, we plant our garden, go for walks, and try to be outside as much as possible to enjoy the newly warm weather. And when summer rolls around, we do it all again.

But our lives have seasons to them too. Depending on where you are in your stage of life, or even in a given year, different aspects of your life will look different from one season to the next. The Bible talks about the importance of seasons in Ecclesiastes 3.

> *There is a time for everything,*
> *and a season for every activity under the heavens:*
> *a time to be born and a time to die,*
> *a time to plant and a time to uproot,*
> *a time to kill and a time to heal,*
> *a time to tear down and a time to build,*
> *a time to weep and a time to laugh,*
> *a time to mourn and a time to dance,*
> *a time to scatter stones and a time to gather them,*
> *a time to embrace and a time to refrain from embracing,*
> *a time to search and a time to give up,*
> *a time to keep and a time to throw away,*
> *a time to tear and a time to mend,*
> *a time to be silent and a time to speak,*
> *a time to love and a time to hate,*
> *a time for war and a time for peace.*

It's easy to let the season you're in define not only how you feel, but also who you are. You might be in a season of working like crazy building your career, but that doesn't mean you're a work-aholic. You might be in a season of staying home with your kids full time, but that doesn't mean you're "just a mom." You might be struggling or scraping pennies together to get by, but these are examples of *where* you are, not *who* you are. You are not the season you're in. In this third stage of getting back to you, we're going to spend ten days exploring what season of life you're in and how that affects different parts of your life: from your family to your home, from your money to your priorities, and more. Now that we've refocused on who God is and who you are in him, you can find strength and grace for the season you're in right now—regardless of what it might look like.

Your Season of Work

"I know that there is nothing better for people than to
be happy and to do good while they live. That each of
them may ... find satisfaction in all their toil—this is
the gift of God.... There is nothing better for a person
than to enjoy their work."
—ECCLESIASTES 3:12–13, 22

I had just gotten home from work, and I was on the verge
of losing it. I worked insane hours at the YMCA and was
on call 24/7 if something went wrong. Since the YMCA was open
104 hours per week, and I managed a staff of two hundred teenagers, something was *always* going wrong. My nerves were shot.
When my phone would ring, my heart would race before I even
looked to see who it was. Because let's be honest, I always knew
who it was.

On this particular day, I walked into the house, threw my bag down, and said to my roommate, "I can't do this anymore. I'm exhausted. I never get a break." And right as my voice began to crack and tears welled up in my eyes, my cell phone started ringing. I winced at the sound and answered it. Someone dove into the shallow end of the pool and hit their head. They seemed okay, but the lifeguards had to treat it as a spinal injury. The ambulance had been called. I was back out the door on my way back to work. Again.

I dealt with life-threatening injuries, teenage staff members making out, and massive drums of extremely dangerous chemicals. This was all in addition to the normal daily problems: Someone was always having an accident in the pool, someone was always late to work, and someone was always complaining about something. It was nonstop—and I was only twenty-three!

The years I spent working at the YMCA were rewarding and fulfilling in so many ways. But they were also full of exhaustion, burnout, and breakdowns. More than once I asked myself, like Jack Nicholson, *Is this really as good as it gets?*

What I know now that I didn't know then is that it was a season—a season of career building and preparation. It wasn't forever, and it wasn't a reflection of who I was or would always be.

We were all created to work in some capacity—or "toil" as Ecclesiastes says—but it's very easy to look for labels to define who we are by what we do. When we meet someone new, it's often the first question we ask to figure out who this new person is: "So, what do you do?" It's also the first reference point we use for figuring out who *we* are. This can be a source of pride and fulfilment if we love what we do. And it can be a source of shame or frustration if we don't. But you are more than your work, and you are more than anything that you do or don't do.

Maybe you're in a season of working like crazy trying to get your career off the ground, and you're tired. Maybe you're in a season of working in a job (or two or three!) you hate just to provide for your family, and you're unhappy. Maybe you've decided to stay home with your kids, and you're feeling a little unfulfilled. Here's the key: This season is *where* you are, not *who* you are. Once you realize that, it's easier to find grace and strength to get through it.

This season is where *you are, not* who *you are.*

So when your phone sends your heart racing, or you want to run out the door because your kids are driving you crazy, or you want to quit because your boss is breathing down your neck, or you just feel overwhelmed and unfulfilled, remember: This is a season. It won't last forever. I believe God has something for you right where you are, and if you trust him, he'll not only sustain you in this season, he'll also prepare you for the next one.

REFLECTION AND PRAYER

*What season of work are you in right now? What
types of emotions does that bring up? Do you feel
satisfied and fulfilled with how you're using your gifts
and talents, or do you sense an urging to look for
something different? If you need to make a change,
what are some of the first steps you need to take?*

*Spend some time in prayer today asking God what
he wants you to do. God has a lot to say about work,
and he cares deeply about how you manage your
talents, gifts, skills, and time. Ask him to help you
be faithful where you are while also having wisdom
to discern what he might have for you next.*

Your Season of Love

" 'Teacher, which is the greatest commandment in the Law?' Jesus replied: 'Love the Lord your God with all your heart and with all your soul and with all your mind. This is the first and greatest commandment.'"
—MATTHEW 22:36–38

August 1 was the day Matt asked me to get ice cream and hang out. In many ways, it was the beginning of our forever. But what I didn't mention before is that as my eyes opened to the amazing man in front of me, something else happened.

I had this very, *very* strong sense that I was not supposed to date him. I know. Crazy, right? It was like God was showing me how incredible Matt was while simultaneously saying, "But you can't have him." It felt cruel.

I felt conflicted and sick with sadness, but after dating Matt for three weeks, I couldn't fight it any longer. I knew I had to end it. I had no idea why, but God's instructions were insanely clear and annoyingly persistent: The answer was no.

I remember sitting in Matt's old SUV in front of my rental house sobbing as I tried to explain: "I don't know why God is doing this. I think you're the most wonderful man I've ever met. And God is telling me no. It's not fair. I'm so sorry."

And then I said these words I'll never forget: "But if God is making me choose between you and him, I have to choose him."

---

*If God is making me choose between you
and him, I have to choose him.*

I got out of the car, and that was it. It was over, and I didn't understand. I cried some more.

Matt and I kept in touch as friendly acquaintances the next couple of weeks. Then one night, he came over to bring me something, and we both noticed something was different. It was as if, out of nowhere, God was blessing the relationship. We were both a little awkward, very cautious, and silently confused as to what was happening. As crazy as it sounds, it was as if the off-limits mandate had been inexplicably lifted, and we were free to be together again. Something shifted, and while we didn't understand it, we were so grateful.

And *that* was the beginning of forever. Matt and I dated for a little over a year, were engaged for six months, and have been married since 2012. Later, when we talked about our breakup, I asked him, "What *was* that? I know God was asking me to choose him, but why did he let us be together in the end?"

Matt said, "I think it was like Abraham and Isaac. Abraham went all the way to raising the knife. Then, and only then—once he'd proven faithful—did God bless him. God wanted to know if you'd go through with it. Anyone can say, 'Sure, God. I choose you over a man.' But he wanted you to feel it."

Yes. That was exactly what it was.

I remember telling my mentor Eve this story shortly after it happened: "I had to choose God. I had to show that I would choose him before he would let me have the man who would become my husband." And Eve's response was brilliant. She said, "You don't have to do it once, Christy. You have to do it over and over for the rest of your life."

Having been married eight years now, I can say that is 100 percent true. It's so easy to choose the living, breathing human in front of you. To lean on him instead of God. Now, Matt is amazing and marriage is awesome. But Matt is not God, and marriage isn't supposed to be an idol. Everyone's story is different, but married or not, God wants our hearts.

So regardless of your season of love, I want you to know that God wants your heart. He wants it first, and he wants it the most. Right now—today—I pray you can find a safe place of rest, comfort, and love in the God who created you. And when he's ready, he will write the next chapter of your love story. Remember, he knows everything, he can do anything, he is for you, and he is always, always on time.

REFLECTION AND PRAYER

What season of love are you in right now? How does this season make you feel about yourself? What do you sense God is showing you in this season?

Spend some time in prayer today asking God to draw you near to him in this season. Ask him to hold your heart in his hands, to surround you with his presence, and to embrace you with his perfect love.

Your Season of Children and Legacy

"I am the vine; you are the branches. If you remain in me and I in you, you will bear much fruit; apart from me you can do nothing."

—John 15:5

*M*otherhood is hard. I don't mean being a mom and raising kids, even though that's hard too. I mean the topic of motherhood is hard. It's really, really hard. I think it's one of the most delicate, sensitive, personal, and emotionally charged topics in our culture.

For example, on Mother's Day, and every day, I want to honor my friends who are moms. I want to celebrate all of the ways I learn from them and am thankful to get to do life with them. I want to celebrate my own mom and thank her for her love and sacrifice for me and the other women who have mothered me as well. Motherhood is exhausting and insanely difficult, and I think it's awesome that it's celebrated. If you're a mom, I want you to know that you're amazing, and I want you to *enjoy* being celebrated.

And.

And at the same time, I want to be sensitive to those who don't find joy on that day and have had their heart broken in some way. Whether it's infertility, a loss, a tragedy, or something else just as painful, there are countless women walking around every day carrying the heavy burden of that heartbreak. I know some of them personally, and I've cried with them on their journey. I don't know why God can seem so unfair sometimes. If that's you, I want you to know that you're amazing too.

The feelings around this topic are vast and varied. Everyone's story with children is unique, but I've noticed a theme in how we talk about it. We often only focus on the outcome—the "having kids" part: Who has kids and who doesn't. How many kids they have. How many are biological or adopted. The genders, ages, and metrics of success in school and sports. It's not that those things aren't important, but if we're not careful, we can spend our lives obsessing over them.

As I was thinking and praying about our focus today, I felt the Lord put John 15:5 on my heart. Interestingly, it's not explicitly about the importance of legacy or children. It says, *"I am the vine;*

you are the branches. If you remain in me and I in you, you will bear much fruit; apart from me you can do nothing."

Think about this verse in the context of children. Whether we have kids or not, and regardless of their ages or stages, we tend to obsess over the fruit. Counting the fruit. Checking the color and shape and size of the fruit. Comparing the fruit to other people's fruit. But this verse tells us to look somewhere else. Stop obsessing over the outcome—the children, legacy, and impact that we desire—and instead focus on the source. *"Remain in me,"* Jesus said. *"If you remain in me and I in you, you will bear much fruit."* Do you hear that? If you remain in him, you will leave a legacy. If you remain in him, you will make an impact. If you remain in him, you will bear fruit.

And the fruit may look different than you expected. I've watched Lisa Harper, who I mentioned on Day 5, mother her adopted daughter, Missy, as a single mom. I've seen firsthand the fruit of Shelley Giglio as she has mothered literally hundreds of thousands of young girls and women through her ministries. I've been mothered by my own mom, my mother-in-law, the mom of my best friend in high school, my mentor Eve, and countless other women. I've mothered my own children, and I've mothered young women through Young Life.

This verse reminds us that it's not always about what the fruit looks like. It's not about where it comes from or what shape and size it is, or if it's what we had in mind and hoped for. This verse points us to the vine, Jesus. This verse points us to the source of our comfort and hope, and also the source of our impact and legacy. My hope for all of us, whether we have kids or not, is that we would do everything we can to remain in Jesus. When we remain in him, we *will* bear fruit in our lives.

REFLECTION AND JOURNAL

How do you feel about your own personal journey with children and legacy? How does it shift your perspective when you focus on the vine instead of the fruit?

Spend some time in prayer today asking God to help you remain in him. Ask him to help you bear the fruit he wants for you and then be able to recognize the gift of that fruit—even if it doesn't look like you thought it would.

Your Season of Family

"Why do you look at the speck of sawdust in your brother's eye and pay no attention to the plank in your own eye?"
—MATTHEW 7:3

I was so mad at her. I was pregnant at the time, and admittedly, I got irritated easily. But it seemed like my mom could push my buttons like no one else could. We were at the YMCA, and I asked her to stay right outside the restroom with my boys before soccer practice started, but when I came out, she wasn't there.

Heat flooded my face, and I felt my anger rising. I called her cell, but she didn't answer—and that only made me more mad. I was the coach of the soccer team and needed to get to the fields to start practice. I didn't know where they had gone, and fears flooded my mind. My heart was racing, and my pregnancy hormones were raging.

After nearly ten nerve-wracking minutes of me running through every part of the building and parking lot looking for them, my phone rang. It was her.

"*WHERE ARE YOU?*" I shouted into the phone.

"What? We're at the soccer field."

When I finally got to her, I said through clenched teeth, "I asked you to stay right outside the bathroom."

"I didn't hear you," she said.

Angry from having heard that same response for years, I said, "You have ears. You can hear fine. *You don't listen.* It's a very big difference."

I'm not proud of what I said to my mom. I'm very grateful she's so involved in the daily life of my children—and I wish I had been more kind. And while I wish our fight was a rare occurrence, the truth is that my mom and I have had countless fights over the years. We love each other like crazy, and we drive each other crazy. That's family. It's complicated. It's wonderful. And it's really hard.

About a week after that happened, I was reading *Discerning the Voice of God* by Priscilla Shirer. The chapter was all about listening for God. As I closed the book, I felt that familiar voice again: *You have ears, Christy. You can hear fine. You don't listen.*

Ouch.

It was completely loving, but like we talked about on Day 8, God will tell you the truth. And nothing puts you in your place quite like God speaking your own words back to you. In that moment, I realized I do the very thing my mom does. The thing that drives me crazy about her—the thing I'm just as guilty of.

You have ears, Christy. You can hear fine. You don't listen.

Family is complicated. Even though they may all be wonderful people, it can still be so hard to navigate the relationships, expectations, and baggage that every person brings to the table. But this devotional isn't about how to fix your family. It's about how to get back to you.

I can't control my mom or anyone else in my family—and neither can you. But as Matthew 7:3 reminds us: We can control ourselves. We can't control the speck in their eye, but we can control what's in ours. You're not wrong to be frustrated when your mom ignores your request or when your mother-in-law is passive-aggressive. You're a grown woman, and you need to set boundaries, communicate clearly, and lead your part of the relationship. But before you start spitting out well-timed lines that make you feel better and the other person feel bad, take a moment to look in the mirror. Check your eyes for specks and planks. And while you're at it, check your ears. God might just have some wisdom for you if you stop to listen.

REFLECTION AND PRAYER

What aspect of your family is most stressful for you? Why is that? How can you protect yourself, and at the same time, still honor your family?

Spend some time in prayer today asking God to show you where you can grow in your family relationships. Ask him to give you wisdom and discernment for how to navigate difficult situations with wisdom and grace.

Your Season of Friendship

"The righteous choose their friends carefully,
but the way of the wicked leads them astray."
—PROVERBS 12:26

I walked in the door with my shoulders hung down and my brow furrowed. My husband immediately asked, "What's wrong? How was coffee?"

I had gone to coffee with an acquaintance/friend, and I'd left discouraged. Again. I'd known her a while, but it seemed like over the last couple of years, she'd changed. Every time I was around her now, I left feeling bad about myself. She wasn't directly mean or malicious, but every other comment out of her mouth was a rude remark about me or another person. It started out subtle but became a consistent pattern.

Once I realized what was going on, it actually reminded me of a funny scene from the movie *Bridget Jones: The Edge of Reason*. In this scene, Bridget is having dinner at a restaurant with friends, and one of them looks over Bridget's shoulder at a tall woman coming up behind her. She whispers to Bridget frantically, "Jellyfisher alert! Jellyfisher alert!" Bridget turns around and sees the woman coming toward her. Her narrating voice-over to the audience starts up again: "Janey Osborne. Talking to her is like swimming in a sea and being stung repeatedly by enormous jellyfish."

Then Janey appears behind Bridget and begins talking. There's a jellyfish icon at the bottom of the screen keeping count of the number of stinging statements.

Bridget! How's it going with that divine man of yours? You must be so pleased to have a boyfriend *at last*. (1) Is he taking you to the Law Council Dinner? (2) Oh. Well, I'm sure he must have just forgotten. (3) Better start slimming into that dress. (4) So he's given you the night off to cheer up all your *single* friends? (5) . . . I saw him just an hour ago going into his house with *little* Rebecca Gillies. (6) She's only twenty-two. (7) She's got legs *up to here*. (8) And Daddy owns half of Australia. (1,497 . . .) See ya, babes.

The whole thing is so funny because it hits home for many of us. And unfortunately, that's exactly how I felt every time I was around this particular friend.

I stood in my kitchen recounting for Matt my own Jellyfisher encounter. When I finished my recap, Matt looked at me and said with zero emotion: "Why do you keep hanging out with her? Every time you come home, you feel bad. Stop hanging out with her."

Huh. What a concept.

We are grown women who get to choose our friends.

So you know what? I did. I stopped hanging out with Jellyfisher. And I'm better for it. I think sometimes we forget we are grown women who get to choose our friends. We aren't stuck hanging out with whoever is in our homeroom class like we're still in middle school. We get to choose our friends. And whether we realize it or not, the Bible talks a lot about this responsibility.

> *Do not be misled: "Bad company corrupts good character."* (1 Corinthians 15:33)

> *One who has unreliable friends soon comes to ruin but there is a friend who sticks closer than a brother.* (Proverbs 18:24)

Do not make friends with a hot-tempered person, do not associate with one easily angered, or you may learn their ways and get yourself ensnared. (Proverbs 22:24–25)

Walk with the wise and become wise, for a companion of fools suffers harm. (Proverbs 13:20)

A friend loves at all times, and a brother is born for a time of adversity. (Proverbs 17:17)

We reflect the people we hang out with. Motivational speaker Jim Rohn said, "You are the average of the five people you spend the most time with." But the good news is, we get to choose who those people are. On Day 12, we talked about how we get to choose what we put in our minds. So today is an important reminder that we also get to decide who we spend time with. If you have people in your life who are negative, who tear you down and make you feel bad, it's up to you to do something about it. In the words of my painfully practical husband, "Stop hanging out with them." Like me, I bet you'll be glad you did.

REFLECTION AND PRAYER

How do you feel when you consider that you reflect the people you spend the most time with? Is there anyone in your life who's a bad influence that might need to be kindly moved to the outside of your inner circle—or maybe even the outskirts of your life?

Spend some time in prayer today asking God to help you see the areas of your life where you need to protect yourself. Ask him to help you seek out and surround yourself with the wise so you can become wise also.

YOUR SEASON OF

Friendship

Your Season of Home

---

*"A heart at peace gives life to the body,
but envy rots the bones."*
—Proverbs 14:30

I was standing in my garage, disgusted. Actually, I've done that many times. Our house is older, and while it technically has a two-car garage, the only two vehicles that could fit in it would be motorcycles. Add three kids, countless riding contraptions, old paint cans, wagons, and yard tools, and there's not even room to park one car. *We just need a bigger garage,* I thought.

I was standing there, staring at the abyss of stuff when I felt that familiar whisper catch me off guard: *You don't need a bigger garage, Christy. You need to clean the garage you have.*

There it is. The truth, lovingly calling me out once again.

So you know what I did? I cleaned it. It's amazing how that one act shifted not only how it looked, but also how I felt about it.

We live in a world where Pinterest shows us what we don't have and Instagram shows us what we should be. And if there's any area of my life where I struggle with envy, it's with my house. I sometimes feel like it should be bigger, newer, more impressive, or that if I were a good mom and wife, it wouldn't be so messy.

Have you ever felt like that? The truth is, there are millions of people who would love to have what you or I have. It's so easy to forget we have more than most. If you're in a season of life with little kids like I am—where a clean, organized home seems like an unreachable dream—the mere mention of cleaning may sound like one more impossible standard you can't meet. But that's not it at all. This isn't about cleaning. It's about contentment.

Proverbs 14:30 says, *"A heart at peace gives life to the body, but envy rots the bones."* Look at the contrast between *peace* and *envy*. Envy rots the bones. But a heart at peace gives life to the body.

To me, home represents a place of refuge, of comfort, of rest. And when I come home to toys everywhere and Ritz Bitz crunched on the floor and jelly smeared on the couch, I want to scream and run back out the door. I don't think stuff is evil, and I don't think you have to be a minimalist to be happy. But I do find incredible peace and satisfaction after I cut out, clean up, and care for my home. It's not easy, and it's definitely not always perfectly maintainable. But doing what you can to make your home a place you actually want to go is worth it.

So how do you find that peace and make your home a place of refuge and rest? Maybe it's finally going through the closet that's been haunting you for years. Maybe it's purging your stuff by 30 percent, 50 percent, or 70 percent and breathing a little easier because you have room to move—and you actually like what you kept. It's buying a nice candle and burning it even if you aren't having guests over. It's printing and framing a photo you really love. Sometimes it's as simple as rearranging the furniture or decorations you already have in a new way.

Loving your home doesn't have to cost thousands of dollars. It can be simple steps you take that make all the difference in how you feel when you're there. For example, when my bed is made, I feel comfort. When I can find what I need, I'm calmer. When I have a candle lit, I feel relaxed. My house doesn't have to be perfect, and it never is. I don't have to have granite countertops, and we don't. But just because your home doesn't look like Pinterest, doesn't mean it can't be a place of rest. What would make you feel at peace in your home? Like God reminded me, maybe you don't need more—maybe you just need to take care of what you already have.

> *I know what it is to be in need, and I know what it is to have plenty. I have learned the secret of being content in any and every situation.* (Philippians 4:12)

REFLECTION AND PRAYER

*What areas of your home are the most important
to you in order to feel peace? (For me, it's my
bedroom and living room.) What are the areas
you can let go? (For me, it's the bonus room and
boys' rooms.) Make a list of five simple things you
can do that would give you peace in your home.*

*Spend some time in prayer today thanking God for all
you have. Ask him for the energy and motivation to
take care of what you have—and the grace to let go of
the pull toward perfectionism. Ask God to help you be
aware of and grateful for the blessings all around you.*

Your Season of Money

"Be careful that you do not forget
the LORD your God."
—Deuteronomy 8:11

When I tell my children to be careful, it's always because they're about to do something dangerous. I think of that when I read Deuteronomy 8:11. "*Be careful,*" it says. The book of Deuteronomy says this many times, actually. Deuteronomy is a record of Moses's final words to the Israelites before they entered the promised land, and Moses was reminding them where they came from, where they were going, and who got them there.

It's interesting to think of money through the lens of Deuteronomy. In my own life, I find it easy to forget God when it comes to my finances. I tend to think of my bank account as this practical part of my life that I manage on my own. I've had seasons where my account was overdrawn more times than I can count, and I've had seasons where we had more than enough. In any season we've been through or will go through, Deuteronomy reminds us to be careful to not forget the Lord our God.

So when you're scared and struggling to get by, don't forget the Lord your God. He knows and cares about you and every practical need you have. Like we talked about on Day 5, God is all-powerful. He's able to provide for you in practical, tangible ways that would blow your mind if you're willing to bring your requests to him and trust him. He still isn't that genie in a bottle always giving you exactly what you want. And it's still important for you to be smart with your money. But don't think for a minute that God can't rescue you—even in practical ways like providing for a bill that's due.

Matthew 7:11 reminds us, *"If you, then, though you are evil, know how to give good gifts to your children, how much more will your Father in heaven give good gifts to those who ask him!"* Don't forget that God knows, he cares, and he can. When you're in a season of struggling financially, be careful that you don't forget the Lord your God. *"And my God will meet all your needs according to the riches of his glory in Christ Jesus"* (Philippians 4:19).

And then when you're in a season of abundance and have more than you hoped for and are living in the fulfillment of answered prayers, be careful not to forget the Lord your God. Deuteronomy 8 continues with:

Be careful that you do not forget the LORD your God,
failing to observe his commands, his laws and his
decrees.... Otherwise, when you eat and are satisfied,
when you build fine houses and settle down, and when
your herds and flocks grow large and your silver and
gold increase and all you have is multiplied, then your
heart will become proud and you will forget the LORD
your God, who brought you out of Egypt, out of the
land of slavery.... You may say to yourself, "My power
and the strength of my hands have produced this
wealth for me." But remember the LORD your God, for
it is he who gives you the ability to produce wealth.

I've been there too, thinking that whatever I have is something I alone produced. But in either situation—seasons of abundance or seasons of struggle—God is reminding us to remember him. He's the first one you should run to when you're in need and the first one you should praise when you have plenty. As Psalm 24:1 reminds us, it all belongs to him anyway: *"The earth is the LORD's, and everything in it, the world, and all who live in it."* Whatever season you might be in with money, *"Be careful that you do not forget the LORD your God."*

REFLECTION AND PRAYER

What season are you in financially right now? What do you sense God is teaching you through the words in Deuteronomy: "Be careful that you do not forget the Lord your God"?

Spend some time in prayer today asking God to show you how you can trust and honor him with your finances. Ask him for opportunities to be faithful, grateful, and generous with your money, regardless of the season you're in.

DAY 28

Your Season of Priorities

"'Come, follow me,' Jesus said."
—MATTHEW 4:19

"*I* need help staying motivated to reach my business goals . . ."

Her question appeared on my computer screen, and I began to read it out loud to the group. This was during a live video coaching session, and I was answering questions from our Business Boutique Academy members. During these sessions, the questions pour in on the screen. I read them out loud to the group quickly and answer them as efficiently as possible to get through as many as I can.

I kept reading: "I'm having trouble reaching my goals and staying focused. I'm falling short and so frustrated with myself."

And then I read the line that stopped me in my tracks: "I've just been diagnosed with cancer, and I need help getting back on track with my business goals."

I stopped reading. I stopped speaking. My throat tightened, and my eyes began to burn.

Cancer.

This woman had just been diagnosed with cancer, and she was asking how to reach her business goals. I was live and the clock was ticking. I started to speak, but the words wouldn't come out. I waited a few seconds and tried again.

"I'm so sorry," I said while fighting back tears. "I'm so sorry you're going through that."

Maybe, and hopefully, you've never experienced something as extreme or as devastating as what she was going through. But we've all experienced change, and so many times, we can hold too tightly to the way things were. Instead of adjusting to the new, we hold our feet to the fire anyway. We want to push through. We want to succeed. The situation changed, the variables changed, the reason we started the thing may have even changed, but we insist on pressing forward anyway. We want to reach the goal or complete the plan we had before *that happened*.

Whether it's a devastating diagnosis or just a call from school that your child is sick, things can come your way every day that will shift your priorities. Sometimes your priorities shift when something more important happens—like a health concern. Sometimes your priorities shift when a new opportunity opens up. Sometimes your priorities shift when God simply calls you.

One of the most famous examples of this in the New Testament is when Jesus called his disciples.

As Jesus was walking beside the Sea of Galilee, he saw two brothers, Simon called Peter and his brother Andrew. They were casting a net into the lake, for they were fishermen. "Come, follow me," Jesus said, "and I will send you out to fish for people." At once they left their nets and followed him.

Going on from there, he saw two other brothers, James son of Zebedee and his brother John. They were in a boat with their father Zebedee, preparing their nets. Jesus called them, and immediately they left the boat and their father and followed him (Matthew 4:18–22).

One moment, Peter, Andrew, James, and John were fishing, completely focused on their occupation and current priority: catching fish. In the next moment, they were following Jesus and completely focused on where he was taking them.

This happens to all of us. Your priorities and goals will shift for a variety of reasons. Instead of pressuring yourself to continue to complete the thing that was important last week or last month, I want to encourage you to adapt your priorities to the season you're in. Listen to where God is leading you and give yourself grace for the changes you're going through.

Jesus called them, and immediately they left . . . and followed him. (Matthew 4:21–22)

REFLECTION AND PRAYER

What are your priorities right now in this season? If you haven't stopped to think about it, do that now. Make a list of what's most important to you.

Spend some time in prayer today asking God to show you what your priorities should be right now and adjust your list as needed. Ask God for the discernment and direction you need as well as the discipline to follow through. Ask him to help you accept grace when things change and for a willingness to drop everything and follow where he's leading.

Your Season of Commitments

"Am I now trying to win the approval of human beings, or of God? Or am I trying to please people? If I were still trying to please people, I would not be a servant of Christ."
—GALATIANS 1:10

*H*ow did I get myself in this situation . . . again? I kept thinking that as I was driving to soccer practice. I played soccer in high school and on a rec league in college. I coached my sister's team when she was six, and I played on an adult league in my twenties. I have always loved the sport. So when Carter was old enough to play, I immediately signed him up.

About a week before practice was supposed to start, the parents on our team received an email stating that our team didn't have a coach, and they "didn't know what to do."

I know! I thought. *I'll do it!* Yes, me. Six-months-pregnant me. Already-has-two-young-kids, a-demanding-job, a-hectic-schedule, and a-crazy-year-with-maternity-leave-fast-approaching *me*.

Sure, in hindsight, I can see what a bad decision it was. Even more so, two weeks in when I realized my son actually hated the sport. Every practice, he held onto my leg the entire time as I coached a bunch of crazy four-year-olds and begged, "Mommy, can we go home now?" *I wish!*

But at the time, the email triggered something in me I have struggled with my entire life: I love to be the hero. They had a problem, and I, of course, had a solution. I'm like many women who have this Mother Teresa complex.

As I have learned the hard way again and *again,* when you make decisions like this, every waking minute will be scheduled for someone else. You will live busy and burnt out, rushed and run ragged. You will feel like Paul in Romans 7:15 when he wrote, *"I do not understand what I do. For what I want to do I do not do, but what I hate I do."* You'll wear "busy" as a badge of honor, but feel like you're dying on the inside. You'll neglect your own priorities and self-care in the name of being selfless, humble, and holy. You'll end up resentful and grumpy because you're spending your one life neglecting your own priorities and doing what everyone else tells you is important. How do I know? I've been there many times and, despite how much I've learned, I can still fall back into that trap.

I do it because I genuinely think I'm helping others, but I've learned a powerful truth along the way: There's a difference between doing something to be *loving* and doing it to be *loved*. If I'm really honest with myself, being needed makes me feel good about me. It makes me feel loved. Galatians 1:10 asks, *"Am I now trying to win the approval of human beings, or of God?"* We say with our mouth we want to please God, but our schedules often tell a different story.

There's a difference between doing something to be loving *and doing it to be* loved.

What would it look like to say no to people more so you could say yes to God more? What would it look like to clear your calendar and ask God what he wants to put there, instead of asking him to bless the mess that's already there? What would it look like to stop and rest even when the to-do list isn't done yet? Isaiah 30:15 reminds us, *"In repentance and rest is your salvation, in quietness and trust is your strength, but you would have none of it."* Are you guilty of that? I am.

I don't know what season you're in, and I don't know what commitments you're juggling right now. But I want to encourage you to stop, even when there are still things to be done. I want to challenge you to say no, even when you don't have an excuse to lean on. I want to invite you to pray about something before you commit. And most of all, in this season, I encourage you to create rest in the midst of your crazy schedule.

Come to me, all you who are weary and burdened, and I will give you rest. (Matthew 11:28)

REFLECTION AND PRAYER

Do you struggle with overcommitting and people pleasing? What do you think is the root of your need to stay busy? What would it look like to clear your schedule and say no more often? What does rest look like for you in this season?

Spend some time in prayer today asking God how he wants you to fill your schedule in this season. Ask him to help you remember that he's God, and you are not. Ask him for the courage to say no and the confidence to follow through.

DAY 30

Your Season

"And we know that in all things God works for the good of those who love him, who have been called according to his purpose."
—Romans 8:28

*H*eat flooded my face instantly. I stood there on stage with hundreds of people looking at me, and it was my turn to walk up to the microphone. I had had a really hard fall season. In addition to traveling every weekend for work, away from my family, and just trying to keep up with life, God was also taking me through some type of wilderness, stripping me of my pride. Oswald Chambers describes it as the "valley of humiliation." I had been there for months and the hits kept coming. Just when I was at the end of my rope and thought I couldn't take another hit, there I was standing in front of hundreds of people absolutely mortified.

I had been asked to speak at an event in town. The speaker who introduced me was an acquaintance, and she made a hurtful remark about me to the crowd before laughing and handing the microphone to me. No one else laughed, and the awkwardness in the room was tangible. I was so embarrassed. Everyone's eyes were on me, waiting to see how I would respond. I didn't know how to react, and I didn't have time to think.

My face was red, my heart was pounding, and my palms were sweating. It was the typical fight-or-flight response and everything in me wanted to fight. I wanted to defend myself. I wanted so badly to put that person in her place. But by the grace of God, I walked up to the microphone, lifted my chin a little higher, forced a smile, and fought back the tears welling up in my exhausted eyes. I gave my talk, paid a compliment to the woman who had just embarrassed me, and sat down with every ounce of composure I could muster in that moment.

I finished out the event, walked outside to my car, and burst into tears. I sobbed. I was so tired. I was so embarrassed. I was so defeated. I couldn't take anymore, and yet God seemed to keep taking me through more. I sat there in the car and screamed, "God, do you even see what I'm going through? *DO YOU EVEN SEE ME?*" After a few minutes of letting myself cry, I gathered myself together and went back to work to finish out my regular work day.

When I got to the building, I went upstairs to my next meeting. From across the floor, a coworker of mine spotted me, waved, and walked toward me. She came up to me and skipped the small talk entirely. In a whisper full of compassion, she said, "I know this might sound weird, but I really sense God wants me to tell you something. He wants you to know that he sees you. *He sees you.*" She had no idea what she was saying, but I did. God did.

I don't know what season you're in right now, friend. You may be in a mountaintop season, or you may be in the valley of humiliation. You may be happy or having the hardest time of your life. Wherever you are, remember that God sees you. *He sees you.* He knows you and loves you and, right now in this exact moment, he's working things out for you. Romans 8:28 says, *"And we know that in all things God works for the good of those who love him, who have been called according to his purpose."*

I'm so proud of you for making it this far on this journey back to you! And now we get to dive into the exciting final stage of our journey as we explore where you're going. And every step of the way, I hope you find comfort and confidence in the fact that, regardless of your circumstances, he sees you.

REFLECTION AND PRAYER

What season are you in right now? How does it feel to know that God sees you, right where you are?

Spend some time in prayer today asking God to speak to you in this season. Ask him to show you what you need to learn and to give you the patience to be present where he has you. Thank him for the fact that in every moment and every season, he sees you.

SECTION
FOUR

Where You're Going

I was standing in church singing during our worship time, and I couldn't stop thinking about how deeply I desired a daughter. I was pregnant at the time, and I just kept trying to push the thought out of my mind. I've been there many times—thinking about something I feel like I shouldn't want. A daughter. A certain job.

A breakthrough. A miracle. Every time a big, bold desire wells up inside of me, I feel guilty. Regardless of what they are, the thoughts feel selfish. They feel silly. They feel vulnerable. And most of all, they feel like a setup for a letdown.

That day, I kept trying to push those thoughts out of my mind like dirty laundry I try to hide before a guest comes in my house. I kept thinking to myself, *I've got to guard my heart. I just have to guard my heart. I don't want to get my hopes up—and I just have to guard my heart.*

And in the middle of my mental self-coaching, I felt the most gentle whisper that I knew could only be from God: *You never have to guard your heart with me. I know what to do with every desire I have given you, and I know what to do with every broken piece when you're disappointed. You never have to guard your heart with me.*

Tears started streaming down my face. The whisper continued, *And get your hopes up? I am the God of hope. Get your hopes up! Bring them to me. I promise you I can handle them.*

That day was transformative for me in more ways than you can imagine. That moment wasn't about getting what I wanted. That moment was about who God is and how he feels about my desires. Maybe they aren't silly or selfish after all. While we won't get everything we want in this life, maybe God wants us to bring our desires to him anyway.

We all try so hard to protect ourselves from disappointment, to shield ourselves from heartbreak. But God reminded me that he is the God of hope. And we aren't fooling anyone when we try to deny our desires—least of all God, who knows our every thought! We can trust him with what we care about most. Regardless of how our heart has been broken in the past or will be broken in the future, we can always remember that, despite our circumstances, our God is the God of hope. Our trust isn't in our circumstances after all. Our trust is in the truth of God's Word.

As we enter into this final stage of getting back to you, we're going to explore what God has to say about where we're going. We're going to look at what he says in his Word about our future. And one day at a time, we're going to learn to let go of the past, take hold of the future, and cultivate a big, bold faith. Most importantly, we're going to learn to get our hopes way up—because our faith is in the God of hope.

May the God of hope fill you with all joy and peace as you trust in him, so that you may overflow with hope by the power of the Holy Spirit. (Romans 15:13)

You're Going with God

"Be strong and courageous. Do not be afraid or terrified because of them, for the LORD your God goes with you; he will never leave you nor forsake you."
—DEUTERONOMY 31:6

One of the things I loved about my dog Jackson was how much he loved to be with me. It didn't matter where we were going or what we were doing, he loved to be wherever I was. If I grabbed my car keys to leave the house, he would get excited—hopeful that he might get to go with me. When he did get to go, he would race out to the car and jump into the back of my SUV before the lift gate was even fully open.

He didn't know if we were going to the dog park or the vet. We could've been going on a hike, or I could've been taking him to a friend's house because I was going out of town. He had absolutely no idea where we were going, but he would jump into the car with every ounce of enthusiasm he had.

One day when I was taking him somewhere, he had such momentum from running and jumping into the Jeep that he slid all the way to the front, slamming his whole body into the front seats. And then the very next second, he turned around and looked at me smiling and panting expectantly like, "Well, come on! Let's go!" I laughed at how excited he was. And in the most unexpected, random moment, I felt that familiar whisper in my spirit: *Christy, what if you trusted me that much? What if you didn't ask where we were going or question my plans for you? What if you completely trusted where I was taking you and were excited just because you got to go with me?*

The lesson was so clear. Jackson didn't ask where we were going before he would take a step toward the car. He didn't try to approve the destination before he would jump in. Every time we went somewhere, he jumped into my old Jeep and overflowed with excitement. His concern wasn't where we were going. All he cared about was who he was going with. I tend to do the opposite. I obsess over where I'm going and what it's going to be like. I ask a million questions and hold back until I have the information I want.

I read a story in *Traveling Light* by Max Lucado years ago that really impacted me:

The story is told of a man on an African safari deep in the jungle. The guide before him had a machete and was whacking away the tall weeds and thick underbrush. The traveler, wearied and hot, asked in frustration, "Where are we? Do you know where you are taking me? Where is the path?!" The seasoned guide stopped and looked back at the man and replied, "I am the path."[7]

God is the path. It's not about where you're going but who you're going with. Deuteronomy 31:6–8 says,

Be strong and courageous. Do not be afraid or terri-fied because of them, for the LORD your God goes with you; he will never leave you nor forsake you. . . . The LORD himself goes before you and will be with you.

Not only does that mean God is always with us, but he also goes ahead of us.

The future is unknown—and that can be scary. We don't know how things are going to turn out, and we don't have any guarantees. There's a lot we don't know and can't control about the future. But here's what we do know: God is going there with us. Every minute of every day, he is with us. He will never leave us and never forsake us. When we remember that, we can "jump in the Jeep" with the enthusiasm of Jackson because we aren't so concerned about where we're going. All we care about is who we're going with.

REFLECTION AND PRAYER

How do you feel about the future? Do you get excited about the possibilities and start to dream, or do you feel fearful and imagine worst-case scenarios? How does it change your perspective to know that wherever you're going, you get to go with God?

Spend some time in prayer today asking God to remind you that he's always with you. Ask him to help you trust his leading and help you enjoy the journey—because even though you don't know where you're going, you get to go with him.

Where You're Going Is Good

"Now to him who is able to do immeasurably more than all we ask or imagine."
—EPHESIANS 3:20

A couple of years ago, my oldest son, Carter, was going through a phase where he *hated* his car seat. He was around two years old, and the moment he was about to be strapped in, he thrashed and cried and tried to push himself out. Then, while I was driving, he would cry and screech until he was red in the face and couldn't even breathe from getting so worked up. It didn't matter if we were going two miles or twenty, he would scream his head off the entire ride.

There was one particular time during this fun phase when we had an unusually warm January day. The temperature was in the seventies, the sun was shining, and there was a perfect breeze. My husband, Matt, and I decided to take advantage of this gift in the middle of winter and go to the park. It was even warm enough for ice cream, so we loaded up the boys for a family day out.

And from the moment we got in the car, Carter screamed and cried. I tried to explain to him that we were going somewhere fun, but it didn't matter. He didn't understand. He just kept crying and wailing. Through piercing screams, I kept thinking, *Sweet boy, if you only knew where we are headed, you would understand. We're going to your favorite park to eat ice cream—which you love!*

In that moment, I couldn't help but realize how many times I've been like that in my own life. How many times has God been taking me somewhere amazing—somewhere with my version of swings and slides and ice cream—and I'm just kicking and screaming? I'm upset because I don't like how we're getting there, I don't like the seat I'm in, or I don't like something about my current situation. But God is saying, "Sweet child, if you only knew . . . if you only knew that I'm taking you somewhere wonderful."

Jeremiah 29:11 says, *"'For I know the plans I have for you,' declares the Lord, 'plans to prosper you and not to harm you, plans to give you hope and a future.'"* God is taking you somewhere, and while it might not always be easy, you can know it's good. It might be hard to see when you're going through something that seems anything but good. But don't lose hope because you're going through a hard time. Your future with God is good. Remember, he is for you, not against you. His plans are to prosper you and not to harm you—plans to give you hope and a future.

God is going with you, and it is so good.

Ephesians 3:20 reminds us that he is able to do more than we can ever ask or imagine. What are your dreams? God's dreams are bigger. What are your plans? God's plans are bigger. What are your desires? God's future for you is even better than that. He has a future for you that is more than you can ask or even *imagine.* You may not know where you're going, but I can promise you this: God is going with you, and it is so good.

REFLECTION AND PRAYER

Is it hard to hope and expect that the future God has for you is good? Does that voice of fear creep in and plant thoughts of worry and doubt? How do you feel when you read Jeremiah 29:11 and really consider that God's plans for you are ultimately good?

Spend some time in prayer today asking God to help you hope again. Ask him to help you fight your fears with the truth in his Word. And ask him to help you find confidence in who he is and where he's leading you.

Where You're Going Is Important to God

"What Jesus did here in Cana of Galilee was the first of the signs through which he revealed his glory; and his disciples believed in him."
—JOHN 2:11

*W*hen Jackson passed away, I cried and cried. After we had made arrangements with the vet and got home, I realized I didn't get a print of his paw to save—and it wrecked me. It's silly, I know. I didn't have anything of Jackson's to keep and was so upset I hadn't thought of it before I left the vet's office. It was too late and there was nothing I could do about it, so I cried even more tears.

About a week later, I got a card in the mail with no return address. When I opened it, I almost fell on the floor at what I saw.

The vet had sent a sympathy card and tucked inside was a print of Jackson's paw. They had taken a print before Jackson was gone.

I still have that print tucked inside my Bible. God cared about something that to others might be completely insignificant. God cared about this insignificant thing and he cared about me.

Elisabeth Elliot said, "If you believe in a God who controls the big things, you have to believe in a God who controls the little things. It is we, of course, to whom things look 'little' or 'big.'" It's so easy to think that our desires, prayers, or futures are not important to God. As if he's too busy doing more important things. As if there's a limit to what he can do and manage at any given time. As if our perception of *big* and *small* or *important* and *unimportant* is the same as his. But God reminds us repeatedly that he cares about it all.

I love the story of Jesus turning water into wine. Jesus was baptized by John in the Jordan River. Then, he was led into the wilderness to be tempted by Satan for forty days (talk about a tough season!). When he came through that difficult season, he began his ministry, and his first miracle was turning water into wine.

On the third day a wedding took place at Cana in Galilee. Jesus' mother was there, and Jesus and his disciples had also been invited to the wedding. When the wine was gone, Jesus' mother said to him, "They have no more wine."... His mother said to the servants, "Do whatever he tells you." Nearby stood six stone water jars. . . . Jesus said to the servants, "Fill the jars with water"; so they filled them to the brim. Then he told them, "Now draw some out and take it to the master of the banquet." They did so, and the master of the banquet tasted the water that had been turned into wine. . . . Then he called the bridegroom aside and said, "Everyone brings out the choice wine first and then the cheaper wine after the guests have had too much to drink; but you have saved the best till now." What Jesus did here in Cana of Galilee was the first of the signs through which he revealed his glory; and his disciples believed in him. (John 2:1–11)

Can you believe that? The very first miracle Jesus performed was to make more wine for a party. The very first time Jesus showed his power—while other "more important" things were certainly going on in the world—was to help a wedding host save face. What an amazing example of God caring about his people!

God cares about every hair on your head and every dream in your heart. He cares about your pimples, your paycheck, and your house project. He cares about the paw print you wish you had and the wine you ran out of. He cares about the big things and the little things and everything in between. Whether you realize it or not—or feel it or not—God cares about where you're going. Every detail is important to him. And he cares about those things because he cares about you.

REFLECTION AND PRAYER

How does it feel to know God cares about the details and "insignificant" things in your life? When you pray for your future, do you pray with the certainty that God is listening and cares? How would you pray differently if you knew what you were saying was important to God?

Spend some time in prayer today opening your heart to God. Don't hold back. Talk about anything and everything, from your frustrations today to your fears about the future. I promise you, nothing will surprise him and what you have to say is important to him. He loves hearing from you, and he loves showing you he cares.

Where You're Going Is in Your Control

"When Jesus heard this, he was amazed."
—MATTHEW 8:10

*E*lephants are the largest land animal in the world, weighing in full grown at around twelve thousand pounds. Yet all it takes to keep elephants that live in captivity from running away is a small, thin rope. How is that? Well, that rope is tied around their foot when the elephants are just babies. They discover quickly that they can't escape and then they never try to again. So even though they grow into massive and extraordinary creatures that could easily break the thin rope and even uproot the trees they're attached to—they don't. They learned young that they don't have control over their situation, so they stopped trying to do anything about it.

A lot of us do the same thing as adults. Something happened in your childhood or your past that made you believe you don't have control over your life. It might seem like the cards you were dealt are all you have to work with, and there's nothing you can do about it. And since God is all-powerful, he's going to control the future anyway, right? It's easy to take this passive approach to our lives.

But like we talked about on Day 19, God invites us to participate in our lives. We aren't just puppets on a string. We're partners with him, and we have a part to play in shaping our present and our future. I can't explain the mystery of the relationship between God's divine control and our free will, but I can tell you there are many times in Scripture where God responded to the actions of his children. He even adjusted his plans based on their faith and actions.

For example, in Matthew, we see Jesus actually change his plan based on what one man said.

> *When Jesus had entered Capernaum, a centurion came to him, asking for help. "Lord," he said, "my servant lies at home paralyzed, suffering terribly." Jesus said to him, "Shall I come and heal him?" The centurion replied, "Lord, I do not deserve to have you come under my roof. But just say the word, and my servant will be healed."*

When Jesus heard this, he was amazed and said to those following him, "Truly I tell you, I have not found anyone in Israel with such great faith.... Then Jesus said to the centurion, "Go! Let it be done just as you believed it would." And his servant was healed at that moment. (Matthew 8:5–13)

Notice all of the actions the centurion took:

1. He sought out Jesus.
2. He boldly approached him.
3. He asked for help.
4. He offered a different plan.

The miracle didn't happen just because God was present. The centurion's actions were part of what led to the miracle.

We have the exact same opportunity the centurion did. We can make changes, solve problems, and seek help. We can make better decisions and practice a bolder faith. We can learn, grow, mature, and improve in order to make our lives and our future better. You don't have to sit on the sidelines of your life. Your future is within your control—not completely of course, but way more than you think. Take hold of that truth and do something about it. You might just find that you amaze yourself at what you can do.

REFLECTION AND PRAYER

What's been holding you back from making your life better? How does this passage from Matthew motivate you to take action? How does it feel to know that you have a say and a part to play in what your future looks like? How can you take control of your life in order to create a better future for yourself?

Spend some time in prayer today asking God for the wisdom and discernment to make better choices as well as the motivation and discipline to follow through with them.

Where You're Going Is Planned

---

*"There are many plans in a man's heart,
but it is the Lord's plan that will stand."*
—PROVERBS 19:21 (NLV)

*T*thought I was going to work at an advertising agency in New York City, and I ended up a speaker and author for Dave Ramsey. I thought I was going to live on the farm forever before I moved to the suburbs. I thought we were done having kids after our two boys until God showed us that we weren't. I thought I knew where I was headed, but God was directing my steps somewhere better.

I often think I know exactly what I'm going to do and exactly how something is going to play out. And you know what? I usually don't. I lean to the extreme of trying to control everything. I run ahead of God's plans and look back over my shoulder every now and then to see if he's still with me. Maybe you're like that too.

But there's another extreme I've seen in my years of working with women. Maybe you're more like this: Instead of running ahead of God's plan to play Cruise Director of the Universe, you do the opposite. Well, actually, you don't do anything. You sit on your couch and wait—for a sign, a lightning bolt, for the angel Gabriel to appear in your living room and tell you exactly what to do. And until you get that sign, you don't move. You pray and wait and pray and wait and wonder where God is and why nothing is happening.

I talked to a woman once who said, "I'm just waiting on God to show me what to do. I've been waiting seven years, but I'm still not sure." Maybe you struggle with "paralysis by analysis" so you don't do anything. Either we think we know everything or we worry we don't know enough to do anything. And ironically, both extremes wrestle with the same fear: *What if I'm doing the wrong thing?*

Here's the good news: Your future is already planned. Psalm 139:16 says, *"All the days ordained for me were written in your book before one of them came to be."* And like we talked about on Day 32, God has plans for you: *"For I know the plans I have for you declares the Lord"* (Jeremiah 29:11). It's a fact. But the best part is, if you're walking with him, you cannot screw up those plans. You just can't. God is asking for your participation, but neither you nor anyone else can derail what God has in store for you. This is the other part of the both/and equation. We're responsible for us, but God is ultimately in control. It's just like Proverbs 19:21 reminds us, *"There are many plans in a man's heart, but it is the Lord's plan that will stand."*

If you're like me, you can work on slowing down to walk with God so you can be more in tune with what he's doing and where he's leading. And if you struggle with the opposite extreme, you can work on getting moving. God can turn a moving car, but he won't steer a stalled vehicle. Practice taking steps of faith even without all the information. We can all work toward maturing so that we can better discern God's will for our lives. Romans 12:2 says, *"Be transformed by the renewing of your mind. Then you will be able to test and approve what God's will is—his good, pleasing and perfect will."* We can always work toward transformation. But we can do so with the confidence that as we seek God first, we cannot screw up his plans.

Whether you're trying to control everything or struggling to do anything, take heart. God's got this. He loves you, and he's in control. You can walk with him by faith, and as you do, I promise he will not let you go the wrong way. Lisa Bevere says this beautifully: "If you think you've blown God's plan for your life, rest in this. You, my beautiful friend, are not that powerful." Amen to that.

REFLECTION AND PRAYER

Which extreme do you lean toward: controlling everything or paralysis by analysis? How does it shift your perspective when you realize that God has plans for you, and the Bible tells us his plans will prevail?

Spend some time in prayer today listening. Don't feel like you have to talk and don't be scared of silence. Give God space to speak about his plans for you. It might be uncomfortable, but it might just end up being the very best part of your day. Remember, we have ears, but will we listen?

Where You're Going Is Provided for

"But seek first his kingdom and his righteousness, and all these things will be given to you as well."
—MATTHEW 6:33

*I*t was 4:40 a.m. and pouring down rain. I stood in the lobby of the Hampton Inn and tried to focus my mind on anything besides the stabbing hunger pangs as I waited for the airport shuttle. I had been up late speaking the night before and hadn't eaten in almost twelve hours. That would be tough for anyone, but when you're pregnant like I was, you're hungry all the time. As I stood there in the lobby, I reminded myself I would get food as soon as I got to the airport.

Then I got a text: "Your flight has been delayed from 6:00 a.m. to 7:45 a.m." I was exhausted, so I went back to my room, crawled into bed, and set my alarm for 6:15. I finally drifted off despite the hunger pains.

I'm not sure how, but the next thing I knew it was 6:55 a.m. I shot out of bed, my heart pounding, and threw on my hat and shoes. I bolted downstairs to catch the 7:00 a.m. shuttle. I got to the airport, through security, and ran as fast as I could to my gate. I was the very last one on the plane, but I made it.

When I got to my seat, I took several deep breaths trying to calm my nerves. I prayed, "God, thank you for getting me on this plane." And I felt that familiar whisper respond, *I'm going to take care of you.* I fought back tears and smiled at the truth in those words.

As my nerves settled and my breathing slowed, another sensation took over: hunger. It was a deep, blinding, painful *hunger*. In my rush to the airport, I hadn't grabbed any food. And with a two-hour flight ahead of me, that meant seventeen hours without food!

I grabbed the in-flight menu to see what I could purchase. There was nothing. My only hope at that point was to beg the flight attendant to give me fifteen bags of pretzels. I waited until everyone boarded. The pangs continued. I waited until we took off. Nausea set in, and I started to feel dizzy. I waited until we got to ten thousand feet. I was starting to feel panicky. The flight attendant finally came by my row.

"I am so sorry to bother you," I said frantically. "But I overslept, didn't get to eat, and I'm pregnant. Can I have as many pretzels as you can allow? I'm starving."

I'll never forget what she said next: "I have a sausage and egg biscuit. Would you like that?" Before I could even respond, she walked away to get it. I was unable to speak as she returned with breakfast—*her breakfast*. I knew the polite thing would be to decline, but I couldn't. I was desperate. I ate her breakfast as tears streamed onto my tray table. God's words rang in my ears again: *I'm going to take care of you.*

Friends, he's going to take care of you too. Where God is taking you is already provided for. You don't have to worry about the details, the resources, the what, when, where, why, or how. All you need to know is who is leading you. I love this powerful reminder from Matthew.

> *Do not worry about your life, what you will eat or drink;
> or about your body, what you will wear. . . . Look at the
> birds of the air; they do not sow or reap or store away
> in barns, and yet your heavenly Father feeds them. Are
> you not much more valuable than they? . . . Therefore
> do not worry about tomorrow.* (Matthew 6:25–34)

"Are you not much more valuable than they?" Yes, you are. God knows what you need, and he will provide for you every step of the way. He will open doors, provide funds, and even rescue you with a stranger's breakfast if he needs to. There's nothing he can't or won't do for you. So don't worry about tomorrow or ten

years from now. God is with you, and he's already provided for your future.

So do not throw away your confidence; it will be richly rewarded. (Hebrews 10:35)

REFLECTION AND PRAYER

Think of a time when God came through for you in a way you didn't expect. How did you feel when God provided for you?

Spend some time in prayer today confessing your worries. Ask God to help you find confidence in his faithfulness and provision. Thank God for how he's provided for you in the past and thank him in advance for how he'll provide for your future.

Where You're Going Is Prosperous

---

*"'We have here only five loaves of bread and
two fish,' they answered."*
—MATTHEW 14:17

T'd never heard of the game Bigger and Better until I read
Love Does by Bob Goff. I've never played it, but apparently,
you take something you have with little value and try to trade it for
something bigger and better by going around to different people
and seeing what they're willing to give you.

I've seen a version of that play out on Craigslist and Facebook
Marketplace. For example, someone might have a fishing boat,
but they post that they want to trade it for a pickup truck. Matt and
I experienced this when we were trying to sell his 2003 Tahoe on
Craigslist. I got an email with an offer: They didn't want to pay our

(very conservative) asking price but were willing to trade us for—
wait for it—a lawn mower. True story. I guess that guy was playing
his own game of Bigger and Better!

The crazy thing is, when God gets involved in what we're
doing, everything really does become *bigger* and *better*. There's
a famous example of this from the book of Matthew when the disciples wanted to leave the large gathering of people, but Jesus
instructed them to feed the crowd.

> *"We have here only five loaves of bread and two fish,"*
> *they answered. "Bring them here to me," he said. And*
> *he directed the people to sit down on the grass. Tak-*
> *ing the five loaves and the two fish and looking up to*
> *heaven, he gave thanks and broke the loaves. Then*
> *he gave them to the disciples, and the disciples gave*
> *them to the people. They all ate and were satisfied,*
> *and the disciples picked up twelve basketfuls of bro-*
> *ken pieces that were left over. The number of those*
> *who ate was about five thousand men, besides women*
> *and children.* (Matthew 14:17–21)

Talk about bigger and better! Over five thousand people were fed
from a few pieces of bread and two measly fish!

I know that in life it's so easy to look down at just what we have
in front of us—our limited abilities and resources—as our own version of loaves and fish. We look at what little we have and think,

But, God, how? We want to dream about the future, but we have a long list of "buts" in our prayers.

"But, God, I'm not smart enough."
"But, God, we don't have the money for that."
"But, God, I'm too young/old to do that."
"But, God . . ."

And God gently reminds us that it's not about us or our "buts." It's about him and what he wants to do with you and through you. Regardless of how limited you think you are, I want you to know that your future is prosperous. Proverbs 28:25 says, *"Those who trust in the LORD will prosper."*

God has plans to *prosper you*. He will multiply your efforts and make you succeed according to his version of success—even in ways you don't expect. As you think about where God is taking you and dream about your future, I want to remind you that life with God is a game of Bigger and Better. Sure, you might only have five loaves and two fish, but that's okay—because God can feed five thousand people with that.

REFLECTION AND PRAYER

Do you tend to feel like your limited abilities or resources hold you back? How does reading the passage from Matthew shift your perspective about what's possible when God gets involved?

Spend some time in prayer today confessing where you've been shortsighted and focused on your own limitations. Thank God for his plans to multiply your efforts and prosper your future.

Where You're Going Has Purpose

"The Lord will fulfill his purpose for me."
—Psalm 138:8 (ESV)

I've prayed a lot of desperate prayers in my life: *God, what are you doing? Where are you? Do you see me?* From cleaning messes out of a swimming pool to speaking to an audience of one in an auditorium set for five hundred, many times I've wondered what God was doing. I've felt lost, rejected, aimless, and invisible. And yet Romans 8:28 reminds us *"that in all things God works for the good of those who love him, who have been called according to his purpose."*

The story of Tamar in Genesis 38 is a perfect example of this. Tamar was married to a man named Er, Judah's eldest son. Er was terrible. He was so awful, in fact, that God killed him. Crazy, I know.

Well, Jewish custom at the time stated that if a man died without a son, his widow would marry his next oldest brother, and their firstborn son would carry on the family name for the dead brother. So Judah instructed his younger son Onan to sleep with Tamar. Also crazy.

However, Onan was terrible as well. He knew their firstborn wouldn't be "his" according to Jewish tradition. So he followed his father's instructions by sleeping with Tamar, technically, but he avoided the part where he was supposed to get her pregnant. God wasn't pleased, so he killed him too. I know, this is insane.

So, by this point, Judah thinks Tamar is cursed. Every time she's with one of his sons, they die! He has one more son, Shelah, but Judah resists giving him to Tamar because he's afraid Shelah will die too.

Talk about being dealt a rough hand of cards! Tamar had to marry this terrible man Er. Then she's robbed of her opportunity to have a son by Onan. And now she's just being ignored entirely. But Tamar doesn't give up. She's determined to fulfill her role by producing a son in the line of Judah. We might not understand this today, but it was a very big honor and responsibility back then. So when Judah's wife passes away, Tamar gets an idea.

Tamar knows there's one more way to carry on the line of Judah: to have a son by the man himself. This is her chance. She conceals her identity, dresses like a prostitute, and waits on the side of the road for him to pass by. When he does, he approaches her and she sleeps with him. She takes his staff, seal, and cord as payment and leaves. Later, when she's back home and pregnant, she's accused of prostitution. But she shows Judah his three items and reveals that he is the one who got her pregnant. He releases her from her death sentence, and she later gives birth to twins, Perez and Zerah.

What a crazy story! How could any of that be good or have purpose to it? When you look at Tamar's life, you see a lot of injustice, disappointment, and sin. And yet.

Tamar and Judah are in the lineage of Jesus.

*This is the genealogy of Jesus the Messiah the son of
    David, the son of Abraham:
Abraham was the father of Isaac,
Isaac the father of Jacob,
Jacob the father of Judah and his brothers,
Judah the father of Perez and Zerah, whose mother
    was Tamar.* (Matthew 1:1–3)

In fact, Tamar is one of only five women mentioned in the lineage of Jesus—an incredible fact at that time. Tamar is an amazing example of how God can and will work all things together for his purpose. Some of those purposes we see in hindsight. And other times, we never know why.

What we do know is that God is taking you somewhere and that place has purpose. You don't have to feel aimless or abandoned. Whether you're cleaning out a pool or crying in your car or just feeling lost and invisible, know that God has a purpose for you he's working out right now—even if you can't see it or feel it. He knows. He sees you. And he *will* fulfill his purposes for you.

The Lord will fulfill his purpose for me.
(Psalm 138:8 ESV)

REFLECTION AND PRAYER

What did you think of Tamar's story? Is it hard to imagine God would use such unlikely circumstances to bring the Messiah into the world? How can this passage give you comfort when you feel purposeless?

Spend some time in prayer today asking God to remind you that he can and will fulfill his purposes for you. And while you're at it, be sure to thank him for them!

Where You're Going Is Eternal

"And this is what he promised us—eternal life."
—1 JOHN 2:25

or my son's birthday one year, he got a set of little green binoculars with cute bugs on them. He's had them a couple of years now and still loves them so much. They have a strap so he can wear them around his neck and use them any time he wants. The only thing is, no matter how many times I tell him he should look through the small holes, he prefers to use them backwards and looks through the large holes. Instead of the binoculars making things appear larger and closer to him, everything seems really small and far away.

This is the same effect we experience here on earth when we remember the most important truth about where we're going: It is eternal. When we live with the confidence that our future is eternal life, it changes our perspective on this earth in a way nothing else can. In *The Purpose Driven Life*, Rick Warren writes, "The closer you live to God, the smaller everything else appears."

Living close to God changes how we view all of the difficult things we face like pain, suffering, injustice, and dying. Second Corinthians 4:17–18 reminds us, *"For our light and momentary troubles are achieving for us an eternal glory that far outweighs them all. So we fix our eyes not on what is seen, but on what is unseen, since what is seen is temporary, but what is unseen is eternal."*

But it also changes how we view the great things we experience as well. Of all the things we can accomplish or acquire, nothing comes close to the joy we'll experience in eternity. Money, success, fame, beauty, power, and every material thing all pale in comparison to what God has ahead for us in heaven. First Corinthians 2:9 says, *"What no eye has seen, no ear has heard, and no human heart has conceived—God has prepared these things for those who love him"* (CSB).

This truth gives you a confidence about life that can only come from God. Your attitude changes and your assurance increases. I love how Dave Ramsey says, "I'm not worried. I've read the back of the Book, and I know Who wins." We live *from* a place of victory, not *for* victory. We are God's children, and we get to share in his glory.

Romans 8:14–18 says,

For those who are led by the Spirit of God are the children of God. The Spirit you received does not make you slaves, so that you live in fear again; rather, the Spirit you received brought about your adoption to sonship. And by him we cry, "Abba, Father." The Spirit himself testifies with our spirit that we are God's children. Now if we are children, then we are heirs—heirs of God and co-heirs with Christ, if indeed we share in his sufferings in order that we may also share in his glory. I consider that our present sufferings are not worth comparing with the glory that will be revealed in us.

So when molehills feel like mountains and everything appears to be under a magnifying glass, remember this: Your future is secure. It is eternal. You don't have to strive. You don't have to fear or worry. You are a co-heir with Christ and have more to look forward to after this life than you could ever imagine. So as 1 Timothy 6:12 says, *"Fight the good fight of the faith. Take hold of the eternal life to which you were called when you made your good confession in the presence of many witnesses."* Take hold, friend. You already have the greatest gift anyone could ever ask for. Now all you have to do is live like it.

REFLECTION AND PRAYER

How does your confidence change when you realize your future is secure and it is eternal? What would it look like to "take hold of the eternal life to which you were called" like 1 Timothy describes?

Spend some time in prayer today thanking God for the gift of his son, Jesus. Thank him for the incredible gift of eternal life with him. Ask him to help you stop striving and trying so hard, and instead, live from a place of victory and freedom in him.

You're Going to Become More Like Jesus

"Now the Lord is the Spirit, and where the Spirit of the Lord is, there is freedom. And we all, who with unveiled faces contemplate the Lord's glory, are being transformed into his image with ever-increasing glory, which comes from the Lord, who is the Spirit."
—2 CORINTHIANS 3:17–18

*S*o, what's next?

That's what I'm always focused on. Are you like that? What's the next goal, next finish line, next objective? During any season of life, I'm always concerned about where I'm going. But God doesn't seem to care as much about that. As I heard a friend say one time: God cares more about who you're becoming than where you're going.

God cares more about who you're becoming than where you're going.

A few days ago, we talked about how Jesus fed five thousand people with five loaves of bread and two fish. He was surrounded by crowds of people and was healing the sick while also teaching and preaching. The whole thing was full of miracles! I bet the disciples were on cloud nine from being a part of it. It was one of those mountaintop moments for sure.

But look what happened next.

Jesus left and made his disciples get into a boat. Not only is he making them get into a boat and leave in the middle of this incredible moment, but he doesn't get in the boat with them. Matthew 14:22 says, *"Immediately Jesus made the disciples get into the boat and go on ahead of him to the other side."*

In the middle of people being miraculously healed and fed, Jesus not only leaves and makes the disciples go on without him, but he also sends them out into the dark night and violent water by themselves. The winds were so strong that the disciples had trouble rowing against them. Mark 6:48 says, *"[Jesus] saw the disciples straining at the oars because the wind was against them."*

I can't imagine what they were thinking. I'd be thinking, *Did I hear him right? Surely he wouldn't have sent me here? How did we go from this mountaintop moment to being completely deserted in* the middle of a dark night? I would be full of doubt. Full of fear. Feeling completely alone. I would want out. But then something amazing happened: *"During the fourth watch of the night [between 3:00 a.m. and 6:00 a.m.] Jesus went out to them, walking on the lake"* (Matthew 14:25).

During the darkest hour, when they were scared and alone, Jesus comes to them in the middle of the wind and the waves. He was showing his *mastery* over the thing they were terrified of. He was *walking* on the very thing that scared them. And he doesn't stop there. As we talked about on Day 5 when Peter walked on the water, he invites us to walk on it too.

Just like in Matthew 14, you will have some mountaintop moments in your life, and you will go through some storms. And while wonderful things happen on the mountaintops, some things can only happen in the storm. It's in those places where we grow. There's a transformation that happens in the valley, where you come out on the other side a different person. A better person. A stronger person. A more confident and faith-filled person. A person who looks more like Jesus.

And that's really what this life is about. It's not about how many mountains you climb or valleys you survive. It's not about where you are or even where you're going. *It's about becoming more like Jesus while you're here.* As we finish out our last day on this journey together, I want to remind you of that truth. You're going somewhere with God and where you're headed is good. It's important to God.

It's planned, provided for, and prosperous. It's within your control, it has purpose, and it's eternal. But as you experience what God has for you now and journey to the place God has for you next, he's going to make sure that, along the way, you're becoming more like Jesus.

REFLECTION AND PRAYER

When have you personally felt the closest to God—in the mountaintop moments or in the valleys? How does it feel to think that God cares more about who you're becoming than where you're going?

Spend some time in prayer today asking God to show you what he wants you to learn right now. Ask him to help you focus less on the next *and be more present in the* now. *Thank him for the ways he's moved in your life over the past forty days, and ask him to draw you nearer to him and to help you become more like Jesus.*

Conclusion

———————————————

There was this girl in high school that I'll never forget. She was popular and a party girl. She was involved in everything. She was the captain of sports teams, on student council, and homecoming queen. You could just tell she wanted to be everything to everyone. She was drinking and dancing at the party on Saturday night and in church on Sunday. She was, as she would say, "well-rounded."

She was also really, really hard. Her motto was: "Carry cash. Always drive. And don't trust anyone." She was both completely untrusting and completely desperate. She looked for love in all the wrong places and felt the embarrassment and shame that came with that life. She was lost.

That girl was me.

I've lost myself in my roles and responsibilities in life for sure. I've lost myself in different seasons or stages of life that overwhelmed me. But I've never been so lost as I was before I met God.

See, I didn't grow up in church. We went to church on Easter and Christmas—maybe, and even then, only as a formality to celebrate the holiday. But while sitting at a Young Life camp called SharpTop Cove in Jasper, Georgia one night, I heard about God in a way I never had before. I heard about a God who created me, loved me, and wanted a real relationship with me. I heard about a God who gave his son, Jesus, for me. I heard about a God who could give me a clean slate and a fresh start. I heard about a God who knew me before I was born and loved me before time began. I heard about a God who accepted me when all I'd known was rejection. I heard about a God who loved me when I was sure no one else did. And I heard, as I sat there cross-legged on a dingy carpet with hundreds of other teenagers, that all I had to do was accept his love. That's it. I didn't have to fight or strive or earn it. I didn't have to prove myself or get straight As. I didn't have to clean up my act or throw out my short-shorts. I just had to accept it. I didn't understand that but, by the grace of God, I believed it.

The speaker invited us to go outside to spend some time alone and pray if we wanted to. I've always been terrified of the dark. I've always had bad nightmares and can't watch scary movies. But I walked out of that room into the dark woods by myself, with a peace that I can't explain to this day. I walked down the gravel path, using only the dim starlight to find my footing. I found a tree and sat down.

I didn't know what to say or how to pray. I didn't know what I was doing, and I didn't know if I was doing it right. But I looked up at the stars and asked God to forgive me for all I'd done. I didn't "invite him into my heart" like I'd heard other people say. Instead, my salvation prayer simply said, "God, please help me focus on you like I am focusing on this star right now." A silly, imperfect teenage prayer from a lost girl. But it was a prayer that caused the angels to sing and all of heaven to rejoice. I was lost, and now I had been found. That night changed everything. That night changed not only where I would spend eternity, but it also changed who I was on this earth. For the first time in my life, I found myself.

I don't know what your background is or what your faith journey has been like. I don't know if you were raised in the church like my husband was, or if you met God somewhere unconventional like I did. Maybe you don't even consider yourself "religious" and aren't sure how this book got in your hands. Maybe you've fallen away from your faith over the years. Or maybe this is all completely new to you.

I don't know your story, but God does. I don't know what you need, but God does. I don't know your pain or your past, but God does. God loves you, and he wants a relationship with you. He wants you to spend eternity with him in heaven and your years on this earth in relationship with him. As we end this forty-day journey together, I want to invite you to begin a new one.

Whether you feel a stirring in your spirit to rededicate your life to Christ or to accept his love for the first time, or like I prayed on that dark September night in 1998, just to focus on him, I want to invite you to do that right now. Take a moment of silence and just breathe. God will meet you right where you are.

Here are some words to guide you if you need them . . .

God, thank you for this moment. Thank you for open-
ing my eyes to see who you are, who I am, and most of
all, who I can be in you. Please forgive me for all I've
done. Thank you for creating me, for loving me, and
for welcoming me back with open arms. I was lost,
and I want to be found. Thank you for the gift of your
son, Jesus. Thank you for eternal life with you. Please
draw me near to you, God. Amen.

And amen.

This is who you are. Of all the places you've found your identity in the past or all of the labels and titles the world has given you
up to this point, this is who you really are. You are a child of God.
You are chosen, cherished, and celebrated. You are loved and you
are lovely. You are a daughter of the King. That is who you are.

You may have felt like you've lost yourself before and to be
honest, you may feel like that again at some point. But you can
always come back to the reminders here in this devotional and
keep rooting yourself in the truth of God's word. You can refocus
on who he is and remind yourself of who you are in him.

This isn't the end, friend. It's the beginning—the beginning of
a life with God that is truly *more than you could ever ask or imagine.*
I'm so excited for you and proud of you for taking this journey. And
now, I'm praying for you as you take this next step into all that God
has for you. I pray that you feel like you've gotten back to yourself,
and at the same time, are ready to step into a bigger, bolder faith

as the woman he created you to be. I can't wait to see all that God is going to do in you and through you. I can't wait to watch you shine!

Let your light shine. (Matthew 5:16)

Love,

—Christy

Endnotes

1. Louie Giglio, *Not Forsaken: Finding Freedom as Sons & Daughters of a Perfect Father*, (Nashville, Tennessee: B&H Publishing Group, 2019), 49–51.

2. Ian Morgan Cron and Suzanne Stabile, *The Road Back to You: An Enneagram Journey to Self-Discovery*, (Downers Grove, IL: InterVarsity Press, 2016), 10.

3. "11 Facts About Body Image," DoSomething.org, accessed August 16, 2020, https://www.dosomething.org/us/facts/11-facts-about-body-image#fn4.

4. Sarah C. P. Williams, "The Human Nose Can Detect a Trillion Smells," *Science Magazine*, March 20, 2014, https://www.sciencemag.org/news/2014/03/human-nose-can-detect-trillion-smells.

5. Ashley Hamer, "How Many Megapixels Is the Human Eye?" *Science*, Discovery.com, August 1, 2019, https://www.discovery.com/science/mexapixels-in-human-eye.

6. Charles Q. Choi, "Brute Force: Humans Can Sure Take a Punch," *Live Science*, February 3, 2010, https://www.livescience.com/6040-brute-force-humans-punch.html.

7. Max Lucado, *Traveling Light: Releasing the Burdens You Were Never Intended to Bear*, (Nashville, Tennessee: Thomas Nelson 2001), 59.